N

Danube River

BLACK SEA

CASPIAN SEA

Constantinople

Sardis

Ephesus

ens

Aphrodisias

HERCULES

Euphrates River

Tigris River

Palmyra

Jerash

Jerusalem

Alexandria

Petra

Nile River

Antinoopolis

RED SEA

ANTINOÜS

Cover: Hadrian, one of Rome's greatest emperors, is seen portrayed in a bronze bust, against a backdrop of the coffered dome of the Pantheon, a temple he had erected between AD 118 and 128. Deeply interested in architecture, Hadrian saw to it that the Pantheon expressed a new-found confidence in Roman design and construction methods over the Greek models that had long inspired him.

End paper: The map appears on a background painted to look like marble by the artist Paul Breeden. It shows the entire extent of the Roman Empire at its fullest. Icons representing buildings and artifacts mark the areas where they were found. These icons and those in the timeline *(pages 158-159)* were also painted by Breeden.

ROME:
ECHOES OF
IMPERIAL GLORY

TIME-LIFE BOOKS

EDITOR-IN-CHIEF: John L. Papanek
Executive Editor: Roberta Conlan
Director of Editorial Resources:
Elise D. Ritter-Clough
Executive Art Director: Ellen Robling
Director of Photography and Research:
John Conrad Weiser
Editorial Board: Russell B. Adams, Jr.,
Dale M. Brown, Janet Cave, Robert Doyle,
Jim Hicks, Rita Thievon Mullin, Robert
Somerville, Henry Woodhead
Assistant Director of Editorial Resources:
Norma E. Shaw

PRESIDENT: John D. Hall

Vice President, Director of Marketing:
Nancy K. Jones
Vice President, New Product Development:
Neil Kagan
Director of Production Services: Robert N. Carr
Production Manager: Marlene Zack
Director of Technology: Eileen Bradley
Supervisor of Quality Control: James King

Editorial Operations
Production: Celia Beattie
Library: Louise D. Forstall
Computer Composition: Deborah G. Tait
(Manager), Monika D. Thayer, Janet
Barnes Syring, Lillian Daniels
Interactive Media Specialist: Patti H. Cass

Time-Life Books is a division of Time Life
Inc.

PRESIDENT AND CEO: John M. Fahey, Jr.

Library of Congress
Cataloging in Publication Data
Rome: echoes of imperial glory / by the
editors of Time-Life Books.
   p. cm.—(Lost civilizations)
  Includes bibliographical references and index.
  ISBN 0-8094-9016-1 (trade)
  ISBN 0-8094-9017-X (library)
  1. Rome—History—Hadrian, 117-138.
  2. Rome—Antiquities. 3. Hadrian,
Emperor of Rome, 76-138. 4. Roman
Forum (Rome, Italy). 5. Hadrian's Wall
(England).
  I. Time-Life Books. II. Series.
DG295.R65 1994
937—dc20
            93-37766

LOST CIVILIZATIONS

SERIES EDITOR: Dale M. Brown
Administrative Editor: Philip Brandt George

Editorial staff for *Rome: Echoes of Imperial
  Glory*
Senior Art Director: Susan K. White
Art Director: Bill McKenney
Picture Editor: Kristin Baker Hanneman
Text Editors: Charlotte Anker (principal),
  Jim Hicks
Writers: Denise Dersin, Charles J. Hagner
Associate Editor/Research & Writing: Robin
  Currie
Associate Editors/Research: Dan Kulpinski,
  Jacqueline L. Shaffer
Senior Copyeditor: Jarelle S. Stein
Picture Coordinator: David A. Herod
Editorial Assistant: Patricia D. Whiteford

Special Contributors: George Constable, John
Cottrell, Ellen Galford, Jim Hicks, Barbara
Mallen, David S. Thomson (text); Lynne
Williams Bair, Ann-Louise Gates, Maureen
Lenihan, Gail Prensky, Bonnie Stutski
(research); Roy Nanovic (index)

Correspondents: Elisabeth Kraemer-Singh
(Bonn), Christine Hinze (London), Christina
Lieberman (New York), Maria Vincenza
Aloisi (Paris), Ann Natanson (Rome).
Valuable assistance was also provided by
Mehmet Ali Kislali (Ankara), Judy Aspinall
(London), Elizabeth Brown (New York), Ann
Wise (Rome).

The Consultants:
William L. MacDonald, architectural historian
and critic, specializes in Roman history and
culture. Author of the award-winning two-
volume *The Architecture of the Roman Empire*,
he is currently preparing a book on Hadrian's
Villa.

James Packer, professor of classics at Northwestern University, has directed a project to
clean and survey the Forum of Trajan and
make accurate drawings of what it would look
like restored to its original grandeur.

Robert Lindley Vann has participated in both
terrestrial and underwater archaeological studies at ancient Roman sites on the rim of the
Mediterranean, including a major excavation
at Sardis, Turkey. He also directed a survey of
ancient harbors in Turkey and a study of the
harbor at Caesaria in Israel.

Other Publications:

WEIGHT WATCHERS® SMART
  CHOICE RECIPE COLLECTION
TRUE CRIME
THE AMERICAN INDIANS
THE ART OF WOODWORKING
ECHOES OF GLORY
THE NEW FACE OF WAR
HOW THINGS WORK
WINGS OF WAR
CREATIVE EVERYDAY COOKING
COLLECTOR'S LIBRARY
  OF THE UNKNOWN
CLASSICS OF WORLD WAR II
TIME-LIFE LIBRARY OF CURIOUS AND
  UNUSUAL FACTS
AMERICAN COUNTRY
VOYAGE THROUGH THE UNIVERSE
THE THIRD REICH
THE TIME-LIFE GARDENER'S GUIDE
MYSTERIES OF THE UNKNOWN
TIME FRAME
FIX IT YOURSELF
FITNESS, HEALTH & NUTRITION
SUCCESSFUL PARENTING
HEALTHY HOME COOKING
UNDERSTANDING COMPUTERS
LIBRARY OF NATIONS
THE ENCHANTED WORLD
THE KODAK LIBRARY
  OF CREATIVE PHOTOGRAPHY
GREAT MEALS IN MINUTES
THE CIVIL WAR
PLANET EARTH
COLLECTOR'S LIBRARY
  OF THE CIVIL WAR
THE EPIC OF FLIGHT
THE GOOD COOK
WORLD WAR II
HOME REPAIR AND IMPROVEMENT
THE OLD WEST

*For information on and a full description of any of the
Time-Life Books series listed above, please call 1-800-
621-7026 or write:*
Reader Information
Time-Life Customer Service
P.O. Box C-32068
Richmond, Virginia 23261-2068

This volume is one in a series that explores the
worlds of the past, using the finds of archaeologists
and other scientists to bring ancient peoples and
their cultures vividly to life.

Other volumes included in the series:

Egypt: Land of the Pharaohs
Aztecs: Reign of Blood & Splendor
Pompeii: The Vanished City
Incas: Lords of Gold and Glory
The Holy Land
Mound Builders & Cliff Dwellers
Wondrous Realms of the Aegean
The Magnificent Maya
Sumer: Cities of Eden
China's Buried Kingdoms
Vikings: Raiders from the North
Ramses II: Magnificence on the Nile

ROME: ECHOES OF IMPERIAL GLORY

By the Editors of Time-Life Books
TIME-LIFE BOOKS, ALEXANDRIA, VIRGINIA

CONTENTS

The columned facade of the marble library at Ephesus, in today's Turkey, expresses the grandeur that marked the cities of the Roman Empire. Ephesus was a particular favorite of Hadrian's, the well-traveled and discerning emperor who reigned between AD 117 and 138, when Rome's colonies stretched from the Middle East west to Morocco and north to Britain.

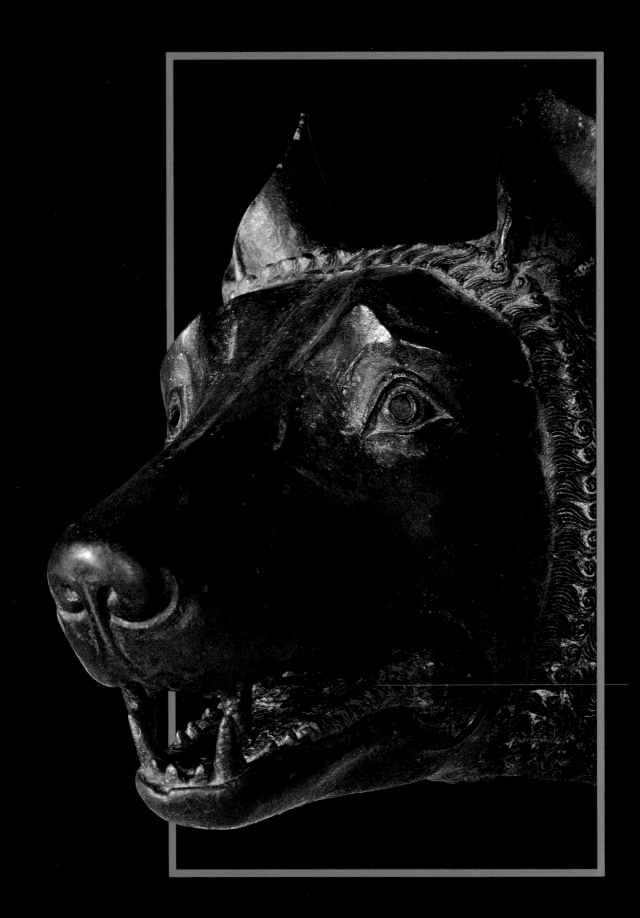

THE ROMAN FORUM: NERVE CENTER OF THE EMPIRE

Beneath the darkening sky of a Roman evening in 45 BC, torches flared in the Forum of Rome. Thousands of people crowded into this great public space, yet the massed onlookers must have fallen—if only for a moment—into a stunned and eerie silence.

Something strange was taking place on the steep, paved incline that led from the Forum up to the lofty Temple of Jupiter on the Capitoline Hill. A procession of 40 elephants parted into two long lines, forming a passageway that was illuminated by the blazing lamps of their riders. Along this corridor of light rolled a chariot bearing the world-conquering Julius Caesar. This was the man who had defeated the tribes of Gaul, won decisive wars in Egypt, North Africa, and Asia Minor, and put down his rival Pompey, who had challenged him for supreme power over the Roman state, in an epic battle at Pharsalus in Greece.

On five days of public celebration, Rome had honored these separate victories. Five times, triumphal processions had crossed the Forum. The soldiers who had achieved these successes for Rome had marched in formation, escorting wagonloads of the gold and silver spoils of war—some of which would, in the course of the festivities, be shared with the troops according to their ranks. In order to divert and edify the watching populace, floats adorned with scenic

A sixth-century BC bronze of the she-wolf myth says suckled Romulus and Remus, Rome's founders, serves even today as an emblem of the aggressive city. From humble origins in a hilly, marshy area, Rome rose to rule a two-million-square-mile empire.

9

displays, depicting the dramatic highlights of these campaigns, moved along the parade route. On the day earmarked for the celebration of the Pontic War, which had been fought near the Black Sea in Asia Minor, the designers of one of the floats had found a simple but effective way of conveying the seemingly effortless nature of Caesar's triumph. Instead of a battle scene, they opted for a verbal inscription, quoting Caesar's own report of his victory: "*Veni, vidi, vici*"—I came, I saw, I conquered.

But the Gallic celebration had been marred by an accident that would strike any right-thinking Roman as a dangerous omen. For the chariot that had carried the conqueror through the cheering crowds had suddenly lurched because of a broken axle, nearly pitching the 54-year-old general headlong onto the ground. Perhaps to deter any evil fate after so much good fortune, Caesar had resolved to cap his triumphs with a spectacular act of public penance. Now, in the glare of the lamps, he dropped to his knees on the pavement of stone slabs in front of the Temple of Jupiter. In this painful posture of self-abasement, he crawled up the steps of the podium, inch by inch, until he reached the very top. Scraped skin and sore muscles were a small price to pay. The reward was not only the presumed approval of the gods but also the public's acclamation of a leader so clearly ready to sacrifice himself for the collective good of Rome.

Caesar's attempt to propitiate Fortune was made on behalf of

Rome's six forums occupied the center of the city and contained many of its most important buildings. The original Forum, bounded at one end by the Capitoline Hill and at the other by the Colosseum, ran at an angle to the five imperial forums, those of Julius Caesar and the emperors Augustus, Trajan, Nerva, and Vespasian.

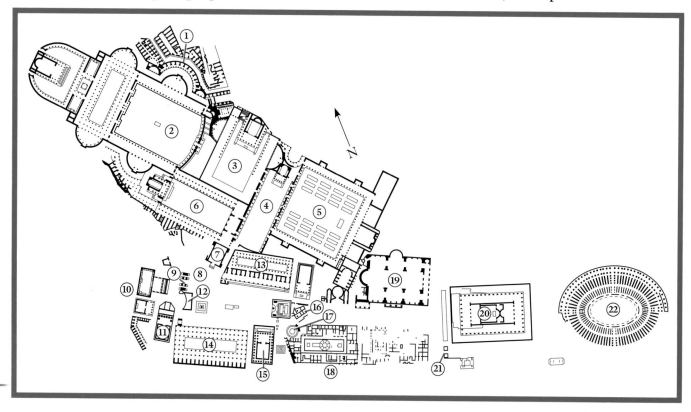

a Rome that still called itself a republic; those who followed him would reign as emperors. In AD 44 one of these successors, Emperor Claudius, tried to emulate Caesar's famous kneeling ascent, without the same prowess. The infirm Claudius had to be supported by his sons-in-law as he dragged himself up the steps.

Long before the age of Julius Caesar and the days of empire, the Forum was the place where Romans came to witness and take part in the great moments of their communal history. The Forum's beginnings seem as misty as those of Rome itself. Rome's own chroniclers assigned the year 753 BC as the founding date for the city. About a century later the Forum emerged as a market and public-meeting place in the location it occupies today. But this was still a time of kings. Then in 509 BC Rome began an experiment in governance that would last almost 400 years: It became an aristocratic republic, guided by elected representatives of its most powerful families. By 168 BC Rome had grown to be the capital of an empire of a span and power greater than anything the world had ever seen. Seemingly invulnerable kingdoms were conquered, giving the Romans dominion over the territory from northern Europe to the coasts of Africa and east to the Euphrates River, where Roman trade routes continued into the heart of Asia. Little more than a century later, the republic was replaced by a dictatorship that, under its emperors, maintained Rome's sovereignty over conquered provinces, while continuing to adjust borders to the advantage of the empire.

In its Forum, Rome would witness the positive proof of this expansion of power, enacted in the seemingly endless succession of triumphs. For Caesar's ceremonial parade was only one of scores of processions displaying the fruits of conquests—wagonloads of plundered treasure and chain gangs of captured kings and their courts. Even the humblest member of the observing populace could hardly fail to feel a thrill of shared success and reflected glory. As the first-century AD author Petronius declared, it seemed as if "the world entire was in the hands of the victorious Romans. They possessed the earth and the seas and the double field of stars, and were not satisfied." Yet eventually the Romans did become satiated with conquest. Nearly two centuries after Caesar's triumphs, Emperor Hadrian, at the apex of imperial glory, would at last come to realize that his dominion had reached its governable limits.

The site of Rome's Forum was wholly appropriate for such symbolically charged public rituals as Caesar's celebrations of victory. The space itself was an open oblong, some 300 feet long and 200 feet wide, lying about 1,700 feet from the left bank of the Tiber River and occupying a low-lying area overlooked by three of Rome's hills—the Capitoline, the Palatine, and the Esquiline. Within its confines extraordinary buildings sprang up for transacting the public business, consisting of law, commerce, and religion. As Rome gained a new sense of itself as a great world power, its public buildings became a commanding expression of that imperial might, reaching ever higher, enclosing ever more space, and exhibiting ever grander decorations.

Although their embracing colonnades and decorative capitals reflected Greek influence, Roman public buildings had their own stylistic nuances. The Romans built their temples upon high platforms, raising up the whole structure as if on a pedestal, in the Etruscan manner. While the lofty Greek temple appeared virtually the same from all four sides, Roman temples faced front with a deep columned porch. This was based on the Etruscan custom of orienting temples to the south, the direction in which the favorable gods supposedly dwelled. For the Romans, such an accommodation served a function beyond religion, however, for an orator could stand upon the porch and rally the populace in the plaza below.

Building on earlier Greek ideas, the Romans began to enclose space in great sweeping curves. For purposes of public entertainment they created bowls and ellipses, such as the Colosseum, scene of gladiatorial combats, and the Circus Maximus, where chariot races were held. They also originated vaulted baths and basilicas, rounded tombs, colonnaded apses and hemicycles, and domed rotundas, whose ceilings echoed the shape of the firmament. And all this would not have been possible without two major developments: the evolution of the arch, which led to the construction of vaults and domes and the invention of concrete. Used sparingly by the Greeks for entryways or passages, the arch became a signature of the Romans. Its strong but graceful curve—still visible in the remains of aqueducts, bridges, galleries, and porticoes throughout Rome and the former empire—found its most peculiarly Roman expression in the freestanding, monumental arch of triumph, built along the route of a victory parade. Such arches drove home to citizens and provincials alike the message that Rome was invincible. Two of these survive in the Forum today, still mighty statements of Roman power.

THE ARCH OF MANY PURPOSES

The Greeks and other cultures earlier than the Romans had made use of the arch in various construction projects, but it was the Romans who took it to new heights. Indeed, through their use of the arch they would turn it into a hallmark of their architecture. They even saw fit to commemorate some of their greatest triumphs with building-size monumental arches, such as that of Septimius Severus above, seen undergoing cleaning.

The trick for the architects was learning how to build an arch securely enough so that it could carry great weight. To this

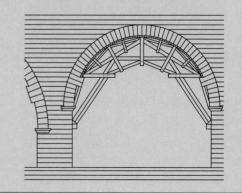

end, masons erected bearing walls or piers and stretched wooden scaffolding and a curving frame between them (diagram below, left). Then, working from either side, placing bricks or stones on the frame, they shaped the arch. Meeting in the middle, they inserted the last piece, the

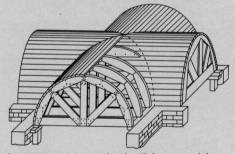

keystone. Now the builders could remove the frame and scaffolding, secure that the arch would hold because of the force of the stones radiating sideways and downward, which was absorbed by the piers.

With the development of concrete, architects soon learned to create taller and more dramatic buildings. They made increasing use of the groin vault (above), assembled on the same principal as the arch, but with even more impressive results, as evidenced above (top) by the great hall of the Market of Trajan.

No one who came to the Forum could escape the message: It was the center of the Roman world. The eight famous roads that linked the city with its provinces terminated here. Close to the Rostra—a stone-faced concrete platform where generations of orators had addressed the populace—a marble column, encased in bronze, announced in letters of gold the mileages between Rome and the cities of the empire. Most of these would build forums of their own—modeled after the one in the imperial capital. Not only would such replications make settlers feel at home in London or Leptis Magna, but also they would testify to Roman authority and be a focus for Rome's civic institutions transplanted abroad.

For the Romans who cheered triumphant Caesar and his legions, the Forum was full of familiar landmarks, friendly ghosts, and half-remembered ancient lore, such as the tale of Rome's founding by the two tribal princelings Romulus and Remus, spared miraculously from infanticide and nurtured by a she-wolf. Sophisticated Romans smiled at such popular fancies. The historian Livy, for instance, remarked that accounts of the city's beginnings were "adorned with poetic legends [rather] than based on trustworthy historical proofs." But the old tale spinners that Livy disparaged may, in the end, have had the last laugh. For recent archaeological discoveries have supported what some scholars have long believed—that "poetic legend" and "historical proof" may not lie quite so far apart as Livy thought.

It might be imagined that the Roman Forum, one of the best-known and most accessible archaeological sites in Europe, would by now be thoroughly familiar ground, with nothing left to be discovered. But new techniques and new technologies have, since the mid-1980s, changed the face of archaeological investigation in Rome, as elsewhere. Because of this revolution in gathering and analyzing data, some of the most dramatic discoveries about ancient Rome and its remote origins are beginning to emerge.

Professor Andrea Carandini of the University of Pisa is one of the innovative archaeologists working in the Forum. In 1985 Carandini began excavating the northeastern slope of the Palatine Hill, at the point where it meets the Sacred Way, the thoroughfare that in ancient times had led into the Forum. Digging ever deeper, by 1987 he had reached the level of archaic Rome. There he came upon a mysterious architectural remnant dating back to the seventh century BC. At first Carandini thought the find might be the hearth that had once warmed the occupants of some long-vanished hut made of wattle and daub. But the site showed few traces of the daub that would have been an essential component of the walls of such a shelter or of holes marking the positions of the wooden posts that would have kept the building standing. Close scrutiny of the soil texture around the structure made him realize that his first assumption was wide of the mark; compacted, discolored earth running some 15 feet in a fairly straight line seemed to suggest a wall far more substantial than that of any humble hut.

The possibility of a wall at this location jogged Carandini's memory. He recalled the historian Tacitus' account of the city's beginning: The legendary Romulus marked out Rome's territory by driving a plow pulled by cattle to trace a sacred boundary line, known as the pomerium, said to have girdled the slopes of the Palatine Hill. Only within the limits of the pomerium could the priests practice augury, the reading of omens that was critical to making decisions. This ritual border consisted of a ditch known as the fosse, beside which the dirt removed was piled up into a *murus,* or wall. Once the boundary was marked in this way, a fortified wall would be built along the line of the pomerium.

Appreciating the significance of such a perimeter, Carandini set his diggers to work with renewed enthusiasm. The results were astonishing: The supposed hearth turned out to be the uppermost, and thus most recent, of a sequence of three stone walls. The lowest layer, Carandini discovered, was formed of volcanic rock quarried from the Palatine Hill itself. An analysis of the ceramic fragments found in its vicinity suggested that this first fortification wall harkened back to the latter part of the eighth century BC, within a few years of the traditional date of Rome's founding. Could this, Carandini wondered, mark the sacred pomerium of Romulus?

Carandini enlisted the help of an American colleague, Albert Ammerman of Colgate University and the American Academy in Rome. Ammerman's expertise was in environmental archaeology, which merges the methods of archaeology and earth sciences to study, among other things, the soil, sediment, and rock found during an excavation. He agreed to search with Carandini for the ditch that would have been part of the pomerium.

Finding the fosse proved a task considerably more difficult than uncovering the remains of the wall. As Ammerman recalls, "At a depth of 12 to 14 feet, we had reached the water table (where the

Exhumed from the rubble and earth that filled it, the 11-by-15-foot study of a house Augustus occupied on the Palatine Hill before becoming emperor was patiently re-created from fallen bits of painted plaster in a 15-year effort that culminated in 1990. Toward the end of his 41-year reign, Augustus proudly said that he had found Rome a city of brick and left it one of marble.

ground becomes saturated), making conventional digging virtually impossible." Ammerman resorted, accordingly, to the methods that archaeologists have recently borrowed from a variety of soil experts. "Instead of using hand augers we bored into the soaked earth, extracted a series of cores, and analyzed them to profile the natural landscape of the site."

Within a few weeks, the search proved successful. The excavators found clear signs of the ditch that had once abutted the exterior of the earliest wall. The trench, it turned out, had been a natural gully that later had been cut and deepened by human toil on a large and necessarily well-organized scale. Measurements have indicated that the ditch reaches a depth of 9 feet and a width of about 30 feet and runs between the northern base of the hill and the Forum's edge. The rubble that fills it evidently consists of material from the old walls themselves, carefully dismantled and used—apparently deliberately—to pack the depression. Not only did the findings of Carandini and Ammerman confirm both Tacitus and the traditions he cited, but they also suggested that Rome, in the age of Romulus, may have been considerably more sophisticated in its social organization than previously surmised. Ammerman had challenged assumptions about early Rome with a previous discovery, this one at the site of the Forum. He had analyzed cores of deep sediment from the seventh-century BC level and ascertained that the terrain of that layer had been a sodden basin. Rising springs, run-off from rainfall on the adjacent hills, and the Tiber River's heavy seasonal floods made it too damp for habitation. Above the moist, peaty, seventh-century soil level lay a drier sediment of rock, clay, and earth. And this layer was a triumph of ancient civil engineering. It was landfill, packed into the basin beneath what then became the Forum. An early Roman king, probably one of the Etruscan Tarquins, had inaugurated this ambitious enterprise to create a communal space out of what had been wasteland.

Taken together, Carandini's discovery of the probable site of the sacred boundary wall and Ammerman's view that seventh-century Romans were sufficiently advanced to organize large-scale public-works projects have triggered a radical reassessment of early Roman history, sparking much scholarly debate. Not only might Rome have been advanced in technology considerably earlier than scholarly convention suggests, but its own ancient memories—embedded in the tales that even many Roman chroniclers dismissed as folklore—may hold more than a grain of historical truth.

An 18th-century engraving by Giambattista Piranesi shows the Forum, then known as the Field of Cows, filled with remnants of the Roman past. The arch of emperor Septimius Severus stands a quarter buried by detritus that all but blocks two of its three archways. The intact building to the left of his monument is the Curia, the old senate house.

However revolutionary they may be, Carandini and Ammerman's findings, as well as the work of their multinational colleagues throughout Rome, represent the latest stage in a long journey of rediscovery. Almost since the moment of its sacking at the hands of Alaric the Visigoth, in AD 410, Rome and its Forum underwent cycles of destruction, occasionally followed by attempts at maintenance or reconstruction. Even as late as the early sixth century the Ostrogoth conqueror of Italy, Theodoric, called his new subjects to the Forum and told them of his plans for preserving the old capital. Despite having been repeatedly sacked earlier, Rome was well maintained during Theodoric's long reign, which stretched from 489 to 526. But by midcentury armies of Byzantines and Ostrogoths fighting over the city left it in ruins.

No longer the seat of multiregional power, Rome decayed. Nevertheless, in 800 the battered city still retained enough symbolic importance to serve as the site for the coronation of Charlemagne, king of the Franks. In Charlemagne's day, visitors to the city could still recognize many of the monuments described in a medieval manuscript known as the *Einsiedeln Itinerary*. Written by a Swiss monk, it was based on a fourth-century map probably created for pilgrims journeying to Rome; the names and locations assigned to important ancient buildings were, for the most part, accurate. The fact that the document still had application in the eighth century indicates that Rome's monuments were reasonably intact at that time. But earthquakes in the early ninth century had thrown down some of the monuments, and the ruins were being buried by garbage and rubble, concealing their inscriptions.

For several centuries more, builders of churches, palaces, and other structures systematically ransacked any portable treasures that remained—gilt-bronze roof tiles, columns, statues, iron gates. Laws forbidding the removal of stone from ancient buildings, on pain of death, were ignored, and thousands of sculptures and architectural elements were burned to produce lime.

As European artists and architects began to rediscover the principles of classical art, students of these disciplines flocked to the Forum, to sketch and survey the surviving ruins. No upper-class gentleman's education was deemed complete without a visit to Rome and its tumbled glories. The 18th-century English poet Alexander Pope called upon these young aristocrats to draw the obvious moral lesson: "See the wild waste of all-devouring years! / How Rome her own sad sepulchre appears, / with nodding arches, broken temples spread; / The very tombs now vanish'd like their dead."

The Napoleonic Wars in Europe meant that Rome was sacked, yet again, this time by the French in 1798. The invaders carried off numerous ancient sculptures and inscriptions. Fearing Rome would lose its lucrative profits from visitors if the attractions themselves melted away, Pope Pius VII established a commission to survey, protect, and maintain the antiquities. The French themselves, during their 1809-1814 occupation of Rome, saw the wisdom in systematically excavating and refurbishing as much of the past as possible and focused their attention on the Forum. Their efforts mark the beginning of careful, scientific archaeology in the city.

Rome became the capital of newly united Italy in 1872, while archaeology, still in its infancy, was turning its attention to this "sad sepulchre." The pioneer archaeologists concentrated their efforts on uncovering the traces of important monuments of the imperial age, only partially buried or lying near the surface. Soon Italian and foreign property developers arrived to capitalize on Rome's potentially lucrative real estate, and archaeological excavation began taking second place to the creation of new streets and buildings. Still, the Forum was partially cleared of rubble, which left it stripped of the patches of greenery that had sprung up between the old stones. The French novelist Emile Zola mourned the results as a "long, clean, livid trench, a city's cemetery, where old exhumed bones are whitening." But Zola might have been cheered by the arrival of the Italian

Pioneer archaeologist Giacomo Boni engages in research in his study on the Palatine, just a short distance from the scene of his labors, the Forum. In the 1899 photograph, boards cover one of Boni's most important discoveries, the so-called Black Stone, which legend said marked the burial place of Romulus. To the right stands the Arch of Septimius Severus, with the ruins of the Temple of Saturn in the background.

archaeologist Giacomo Boni, who launched an important dig at the Forum in 1898. It was Boni's "particular pleasure to heal the scars of excavation by the help of nature," as an admirer wrote, and the Italian duly planted the roses, wisteria, ivy, laurel, and oleander whose descendants still brighten the scene.

As a scientist, Boni represented a new wave in Roman archaeology. He adopted the stratigraphic techniques of geologists in his efforts to peel back layer after buried layer of the Forum's past. The travertine piazza at the very center of the Forum, dating from the days of the emperors, was his starting point. Working his way down methodically through nine layers of earlier pavements beneath it, he finally reached the Forum's first paved surface, a bed of gravel put down in the sixth century BC.

While excavating on the Forum's edge, Boni came upon a mysterious landmark that he identified as the Black Stone, or Lapis Niger. This enigmatic object of extreme antiquity had been mentioned by various Roman authors. The Lapis Niger consists of a covering of black marble slabs atop a stone bearing an inscribed text in archaic Latin, flanked by the remnants of pedestals, some fragments of terra-cotta reliefs, and other small, unidentifiable stone structures and heaps of debris. The text, probably dating from the early sixth century BC, is partially obliterated, and the remnant is difficult to decipher. The inscription's opening lines deliver an unmistakable warning: "Whosoever defiles this spot, let him be forfeit to the spirits of the underworld; whosoever contaminates it with refuse, after due process of law, it shall be proper for the King to deprive him of his property." The archaic language suggests that the stone was set in place close to the time of the Forum's establishment as a public area. Some modern scholars say the Lapis Niger symbolizes the fact that in its very origins the Forum was marked as a sacred and inviolable space, as the heart of Rome.

Boni alone could not rescue Rome from the dangers of modernity. What waves of enemy invaders and plunderers had failed to accomplish seemed about to be achieved by the Romans themselves. In the late 1920s the fascist dictator Benito Mussolini came to power, announcing that his new regime was the true successor to imperial Rome. To clothe the ancient capital with suitably grandiose symbols of its rebirth, he inaugurated digs of important ancient sites such as the forums of Augustus, Trajan, and Caesar. The partially excavated remains were left as attractive vistas beside the newly created street known today as the Via dei Fori Imperiali, or Street of the Imperial Forums, part of a plan that sacrificed potentially important remnants of the past to the misguided fantasy of a would-be emperor.

After World War II, Rome's economy began to expand beyond all expectation. Not only did the city's population explode—trebling in size by the late 1970s—but so too did the rate of car ownership. The Eternal City's thundering traffic began to devastate the surviving fragments of the ancient capital. Every monument exposed to the fume-laden air and the rumbling vibrations began to show scars. When, in 1978, pieces of the great column commemorating the philosopher-emperor Marcus Aurelius came crashing to the ground, municipal authorities were jolted into action.

In 1981 Adriano La Regina, archaeological superintendent of Rome, launched an emergency program to rescue, restore, and protect Rome's imperiled landmarks. He also inaugurated a large-scale program of new excavation, dismantling an over-trafficked street that lay above a crucial site and calling on the international archaeological community to assist his efforts. Today, parts of the Forum and its environs are under the scrutiny of scholars from Britain, Finland, and the United States, as well as from Italy.

While Boni and his 20th-century successors exposed the layers of Rome's archaic past, scholars from other disciplines combed Latin texts for references to its buildings and scrutinized ancient coins, which sometimes bore visual evidence of its monuments. Gradually these researchers built up a more accurate picture of the Forum's layout and of the physical appearance of the structures in and around it. For a vivid sense of the actual sights, smells, and sounds of the place, they turned to the barbed satirical remarks of Roman poets and playwrights, inspired by real-life dramas taking place in this lively area.

In a comedy performed in Rome during the second century BC, the playwright Plautus takes his audience on a verbal tour of the Forum, pointing out the particular corners that were favored by prostitutes, the money exchanges frequented by the wealthy married men the women preferred as clients, the haunts of slanderers and gossips, the gathering places of prosperous and respectable citizens, and the location where loan sharks could always be found. Cato the Censor, a contemporary of Plautus', disapproved of this largely raffish crowd and suggested—apparently in vain—that the Forum be paved with uncomfortably small cobblestones in an effort to discourage idlers.

But many of those who frequented the Forum had good reason to be there. The space had, for centuries, been a place of commerce, with merchants, butchers, and produce sellers in the Old Shops on the southwestern side and in the New Shops across the way. In 338 BC the consul Gaius Maenius had banished these vendors from the Forum and replaced them with silversmiths, money-changers, and booksellers, who specialized in less aromatic commodities. Some food purveyors, however, remained close at hand. Archaeologists have found inscriptions identifying their places of business—and those of florists, perfumers, flute makers, and jewelers—along the Sacred Way, which runs into the Forum from the southeast. Other establishments have also left clues to their purpose, in the form of identifiable floor plans or even furniture. A set of narrow chambers with built-in beds, for instance, suggests that a brothel keeper enjoyed a lively trade a few steps from the Forum's

labored on the model for four years, creating each building on an exacting 1:250 scale. Later, Di Carlo's nephew extended the model, and in 1990-1991, he cleaned and restored it, correcting damage done to it over the years. Because its paint has faded, it leaves the impression of a gleaming city constructed almost entirely of marble when, in fact, much of Rome was built of ordinary brick and mortar.

The Colosseum and the hairpin shaped Circus Maximus, where chariot races were held, dominate the model. To the left of the Colosseum lie the six forums. Snaking in from the right is the multiarched aqueduct of the emperor Claudius, one of 11 such courses that served the city's water needs. The large walled structure between the aqueduct and the Colosseum is the Temple of the Divine Claudius.

northeastern extremity and only a stone's throw away from the most sacred sites in the civic life of Rome.

Chief among these was the Comitium, a circular area 300 feet across at the Forum's northwestern end, slightly below the level of its surroundings, reached by a set of curved steps. Even in the days of the republic, it was regarded as having an ancient history, for it had been the place where Rome's first kings had met with the citizens. Since that remote era, the Comitium had remained a traditional place of assembly. It was there that citizens voted for war or peace, usually ratifying the Senate's prior decision. Modern excavations have confirmed the Comitium's great age; archaeologists have explored seven superimposed layers and found that signs of the Comitium's presence exist even upon the deepest, and thus earliest, of these slices of time.

Adjacent to the Comitium stood the curved platform known as the Rostra. Its name, meaning prows, derived from the victory prizes that adorned it—a number of bronze ships' prows that had been captured in the 328 BC naval battle with the people of Antium.

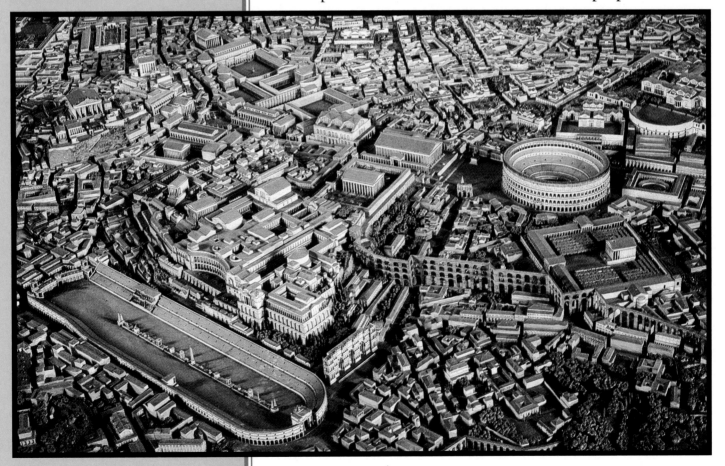

From this podium, orators such as Cicero stood in the shadow of the Capitoline Hill and stirred the populace with potent speeches. Here magistrates issued judicial decisions and public declarations, condemned traitors, and stripped public enemies of their worldly goods.

Julius Caesar dismantled the Rostra and rebuilt the structure nearby. It was from this new Rostra that Mark Antony delivered the funeral oration after Caesar's death at the hands of Brutus. In times of civil disturbance, such assassinated heroes were cremated here in rites that sometimes drove the populace into a frenzy of collective grief and rage. In 52 BC flames from a particularly turbulent political funeral spread from the pyre to the Curia, or senate house, behind it, and burned that structure to the ground. Rebuilding began on the same site, but Julius Caesar soon constructed a completely new senate chamber about 100 feet to the west, where its third-century AD successor now stands.

In republican Rome, the Curia was the place where important political decisions were made. The Senate—the council once made up of the male heads of Rome's most prominent noble families—had existed since the days of the archaic kings and would survive the republic by centuries, until imperial power vanished altogether from Rome. By the late second century BC, this august body included most ex-magistrates who became members after their terms of office; increasingly, during the first four centuries AD, foreigners and commoners joined its ranks. While officially the Senate was simply an advisory body, it gave counsel to the consuls, Rome's two senior magistrates, who were elected annually to govern the city.

Foreigners often were awe-struck at the majesty of the Senate; one diplomat called it "an assembly of kings." From its deliberations came the orders that directed and defeated Carthage in the Punic Wars. The Senate could send armies into action, make treaties, dispatch officials abroad to govern rich and important provinces under its watchful eye, even determine who was the rightful heir to the kingship in a dispute taking place in a faraway land. All this and much more it could do until a succession of powerful generals, including Julius Caesar, paved the way for imperial rule. With the government firmly under the thumb of the emperors, the Senate would continue to function, but with much reduced powers. It had surrendered to the emperor control of the two most important sources of Roman power—the army and the treasury.

Management of Rome's financial resources depended on the

The glory that was Rome fills this 19th-century re-creation of one end of the Forum around AD 200. From left to right are the Basilica Julia, the temples of Saturn, Vespasian, and Concord, and the Arch of Septimius Severus. At center is the Rostra, where public speeches were made. The column to the right is a naval monument, decorated with the bronze prows of captured enemy vessels.

quaestor, a magistrate responsible for the guardianship of public funds. The national treasury resided in the Temple of Saturn, which lay only a few steps away from the Comitium and the Curia on the Forum's west side. Here too were kept the pair of bronze tablets inscribed with the fundamental laws of the Roman state. The tablets themselves are gone, but the iron hinges and holes in the rear wall still remain, showing where the plaques were attached.

By the time a Roman noble took his place in the Senate, he was likely to have risen up a ladder of magisterial and military posts of increasing importance. He might have been a praetor in charge of dispensing justice. He, or his representatives, would have mounted the praetor's tribunal, which stood near the Forum's eastern end, to announce judicial decisions or to send some guilty culprit to the prison at the Forum's northwestern corner to await the death sentences carried out at the city gates in stench and darkness.

The Forum was not only a theater for the wielding of secular power; it was also sacred ground. Since the republic's beginnings, the Forum had been the place where the consuls, in times of crisis, called upon the sky god Jupiter—whose temple crowned the Capitoline Hill—to send them guidance. The heavens were full of portents, such as the pattern of birds' flight or the timing of thunderbolts, that a skilled interpreter could easily decode. In the Forum too stood the

American archaeologist Esther Van Deman strikes a confident pose in the ruins of the Atrium Vestae, home of the vestal virgins, to which she devoted years of study. Van Deman also investigated Roman construction methods and became so astute that she could date walls by tasting tiny bits of cement for telltale ingredients that gave away the structures' respective ages.

Temple of Castor and Pollux, twin brothers who had first emerged as mortal heroes in the lore of ancient Greece and had gradually evolved into gods. According to legend, they had appeared in the Forum in the fifth century BC, in the guise of two shining horsemen, to presage success in a decisive battle. The surviving fragments of their shrine consist of three Corinthian columns of Greek marble. About 41 feet high and set on a 23-foot podium, they tower above the Forum's floor, representing the last remnant of a massive colonnade that surrounded the temple.

Nearby stood the Regia. Originally a simple structure walled in mud brick or timber, it was demolished and rebuilt at intervals over a period of 500 years. It served as holy shrine and official residence of the *pontifex maximus,* or chief priest, of Rome. Well guarded in the sanctuary were 12 large sacred shields. These weapons of war were treated with reverence because one of them was believed to have belonged to the war god Mars; when it fell from heaven, so the story went, an oracle declared that its landing place would mark the center of a future empire. The Regia's first occupant, the legendary Numa Pompilius, was said to have ordered artisans to produce 11 perfect duplicates, so that no enemy of Rome might ever identify and purloin the divine original.

In the Regia's shadow lay another equally venerable, and even holier, landmark—the small, circular Temple of Vesta, ancient goddess of hearth and home. In its shape and design, her shrine recalled the dwelling places of her early worshipers, the simple farmers of the region. Some time before 700 BC, these most ancient of Romans buried the ashes of their dead in small pottery replicas of the round, thatched huts they had lived in, to be unearthed during modern excavations. Visual representations on coins from several imperial reigns and a beautifully detailed marble relief of the temple show that no matter how many times it was destroyed and reconstructed, it resolutely retained its circular plan. The materials used may have become more durable, and more costly, but the poet Ovid's words reminded his readers that "the brazen roof you now see was once of thatch, the walls were woven of tough [willows]." The historian Plutarch reports that the shape of the building was allegedly dictated by the cult's founder, Numa Pompilius, to symbolize the form of the universe itself, with an eternal fire burning at its heart.

Since the era of prehistory, six vestal virgins tended the shrine of this ancient Mediterranean goddess. This elite community of priestesses was chosen from among Rome's old patrician families until a shortage of willing recruits forced the authorities to broaden the field to include daughters of the lower classes and, in times of desperation, those of liberated slaves. Vestal virgins entered the order between the ages of 6 and 10 years, took a vow of chastity, and served for three decades, although records show that some women lived their entire lives in the Atrium Vestae, House of the Vestals. These priestesses had to contend with a full schedule of complicated ceremonial and domestic tasks, hedged about by a thicket of ancient rules and prohibitions. Water, for instance, had to be fetched from a holy spring outside the city and carried home in an awkwardly shaped vessel that could not be rested upon the ground.

Life in the House of the Vestals, with its handsome marble columns, was not entirely austere. The vestal virgins enjoyed privileges, financial benefits, and the highest social status. They had the right, granted to few others, to travel about the city in carriages; they sat in the best seats at gladiatorial games and were honored guests at public ceremonies and private banquets. In 69 BC, for instance, the four most senior vestals attended a dinner party in honor of a newly installed priest of the cult of Mars. The 30-course menu, according to a contemporary document, featured such delicacies as thrushes garnished with asparagus and a dramatic assemblage of pig's head, sows' udders, duck, hare, and fricasseed fish.

Roman historians have provided considerable information about the lives of the vestal virgins, but much of the pioneering archaeological investigation of the cult was the work of an American archaeologist, Esther Van Deman. A professor at Mount Holyoke College, she began her on-site investigations of the Temple of Vesta in 1901, studying statues of the vestals, inscriptions relating to the cult, and the remains of the House of the Vestals.

Van Deman soon took on a full schedule of archaeological activity in Rome, where she became a popular and outspoken member of the scholarly community, unworried by many of the social conventions that inhibited her more traditionally minded contemporaries. Friends in Rome remembered Van Deman as a resolutely unfashionable figure in a beloved but ill-fitting yellow hat. Finally persuaded to buy a new dress for an American lecture tour, she used the garment to wrap up archaeological samples for the voyage home.

Although the vestals had first lured her to the Forum, Van

Deman's boundless curiosity led her into an emerging field of inquiry. She began to study the materials and construction techniques with which the makers of the empire had developed their distinctive architectural style. A key to this new architecture was concrete.

Simpler adhesive mixtures of sand, lime, and water had been used in Crete before 1000 BC and a few centuries thereafter in Greek settlements in the south of Italy. But it was only in the second century BC that the Romans perfected their own remarkably stress-resistant and almost fire-resistant concrete, based on a mixture of water, rubble, lime, and a reddish purple, fine-grained sand known as pozzolana, spewed out by volcanoes. This volcanic ash contributes to the formation of hydraulic silicates, which allow the concrete to set underwater. Concrete was not only easy to prepare and use but also so superior to any earlier mortars that Pliny the Elder could not "marvel enough" at the discovery.

Rome's architects experimented boldly with concrete. Massive foundations, wide arches supported by powerful concrete piers, long arcades, stout concrete walls with thin facings of brick or marble, and vaulted roofs of concrete laid on a wooden centering that was removed when the concrete had hardened, all began to change the face of Rome. Among the largest buildings to employ the revolutionary concrete construction was the Porticus Aemilia, a vaulted warehouse, built around 174 BC and still partially preserved near the ancient commercial quarter, the emporium. After the early years of the first century AD, concrete came to be used for the construction of Rome's enormous public baths, which included gardens, lecture halls, sports facilities, lounges, and libraries.

The city was also renowned for its basilicas. These peculiarly Roman edifices contained a spacious, high-roofed central hall with colonnaded aisles, lit by a clerestory; they were dedicated to public purposes and used chiefly as law courts and as the meeting places of businessmen. The Basilica Aemilia, which had been erected in 179 BC before concrete had wide application, stood on the northeast side of the Forum and attracted Rome's merchants, moneychangers, and their clients, who met there to exchange gossip, sniff out trade secrets, and strike bargains without exposure to the weather. Pliny the Elder, writing in the first century AD, extolled the Basilica Aemilia as one of the three most magnificent buildings in the world.

Across from this commercial edifice rose the first basilica to employ concrete. Named after Julius Caesar who had begun its con-

TRAJAN'S FORUM: PIECING TOGETHER AN ARCHITECTURAL JIGSAW PUZZLE

As Northwestern University classics professor James Packer got ready to lead an alumni group on a tour of the ruins of Rome's five imperial forums in 1971, he stumbled upon a paradox: Although Trajan's Forum was the largest and grandest of these, published information about it proved the hardest to come by. Archaeologists had partially excavated the site twice, in the early 1800s and from 1928 to 1933. But they produced no formal reports, only plaster reconstructions of the forum's west library and of its east colonnade and hemicycle *(see ground plan below)*. Challenged by this lack of information, Packer began a search in archives in Rome and Paris. There he discovered the excavators' field notes, photographs, and drawings, along with 19th-century renderings of the site. These, together with fleeting references by ancient writers and a fragmentary map of

Rome harking back to the third century AD, were about all Packer had to go by.

On the site, however, and in subterranean storerooms and in museums and churches located throughout Rome, Packer came upon the pieces of a massive jigsaw puzzle: thousands of fragments of the marble friezes, capitals, and other elements with which the architect Apollodorus of Damascus adorned the forum. Many of these needed only washing with soap and water to regain their long-lost luster. "They are absolutely in the same condition as they were when they came from the sculptor's hand," Packer says. "After cleaning, the colored marbles are splendid, a riot of color."

Meticulously measured, drawn to scale, and then disposed on paper, such

Statues of chariots on three porches adorn the Basilica Ulpia law court on the Trajanic gold coin at top. Such artifacts, along with the excavated areas shown in color on the site plan at right, provided important clues as to what Trajan's Forum actually looked like.

1 *West Library*
2 *Trajan's Column*
3 *East Library*
4 *Basilica Ulpia*
5 *West Colonnade and Hemicycle*
6 *Piazza*
7 *Statue of Trajan*
8 *East Colonnade and Hemicycle*
9 *Arched Entrance*

An egg-and-dart design and dentils adorn this cornice fragment from the interior of the west library. The piece, carved from white marble, formed part of a decorative entablature or border that separated two tiers of columns.

fragments allowed Packer and his colleague Chicago architect Kevin Lee Sarring to recapture architectural details not seen since an earthquake leveled the forum in AD 801. For instance, they were able to deduce the combined height of the two tiers of columns in the nave, or central hall, of the west library by multiplying the diameter of column shafts such as the one opposite by a constant, then adding the

heights of adjoining elements such as the chunk of cornice above. The calculations revealed that the library's upper tier was three-quarters as tall as the lower—a ratio prescribed in the first century BC by the famous Roman architect Vitruvius.

Armed with this knowledge —and a comprehensive archaeological plan drawn with the aid of aerial photos—an Italian architecture firm turned preliminary

reconstruction sketches by Packer and Sarring into detailed renderings. The one below shows how the southern facade of the Basilica Ulpia must have appeared to those just entering the forum. Cross sections of the colonnades and hemicycles that flanked the piazza to the west and east are at left and right, and Trajan's Column—the only remnant of the forum still wholly intact—looms in the background.

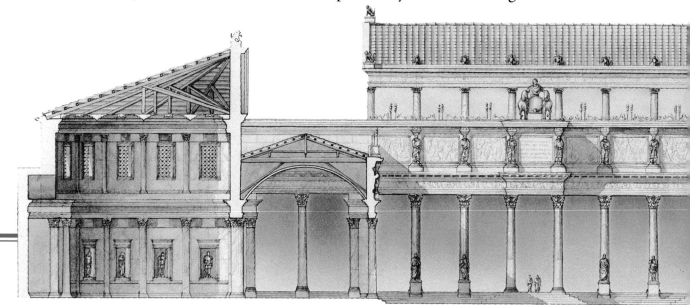

A white marble Corinthian capital, the tips of its acanthus leaves long gone, sits on a fluted column of purple-veined pavonazzetto marble from Asia Minor. The fragment belonged to the lower tier of columns that ringed the interior of the west library.

Wielding a dagger, winged Victory prepares to sacrifice a bull on this portion of a frieze from the nave of the Basilica Ulpia. The fragment, part of an entablature, likely rested upon a Corinthian capital.

struction, the Basilica Julia housed many of the city's courts of law. Concrete vaults soared above arcades at either side of the edifice. Two, three, or more trials took place simultaneously here, with only wooden screens to separate the courts. Curious onlookers packed into the upper galleries by the hundreds, to follow the progress of legal dramas, savor the whiff of scandal, or appreciate the rhetorical skills of the dignitaries who spoke in the course of important trials.

These orators often became celebrities in their own right. Some guaranteed applause for themselves by installing a claque of hired admirers to cheer wildly after they spoke. Others, such as the ex-consul Publius Galerius Trachalus, needed no rented crowd of admirers; his voice boomed so impressively through the Basilica Julia that when his own courtroom applauded his speech, so too did the audiences at the three other trials taking place at the same time.

If the excitements of the law courts palled, some Romans played board games on the grids and circles etched into the basilica's floor. Not everyone approved. Cicero, for instance, speaks scathingly of "a rascal not ashamed to play dice even in the Forum."

The basilica form reached its peak of magnificence, employing all the tricks of the concrete trade, with the Basilica Nova, or New Basilica, about 100 yards east of the Basilica Aemilia, on the Sacred Way. Begun by Maxentius around AD 306 and finished after 313 by his successor Constantine, its architecture was copied from the great bath buildings. If, as some have argued, it was magnitude that gave Roman architecture its grandeur, then the Basilica Nova, 350 feet long by nearly 200 feet wide, could not be faulted on this score. The magnificent groined vault of its enormous nave, flanked on either side by three barrel-vaulted chambers, soared 115 feet above the marble floor. Its massive vaults were borne on concrete piers located behind 47-foot marble Corinthian columns.

Implementing part of a grand master plan he never lived to see completed, Julius Caesar broke with tradition by creating an entirely new and separate forum. It was necessary to augment the constricted space in the old Forum, which by the late first century BC was insufficient for the enormous volume of business generated by the empire. His successors, over the next 150 years, would follow his example by constructing forums of their own. And each new venture drew more of the life of the city away from its ancient heart.

Trajan's Column—a spiraling band of reliefs carved in marble and commemorating the emperor's deeds—rises freshly cleaned from the ruins of his grand forum. The cleaning, begun in 1981, took nine years to complete. The 100-foot-tall column, which is hollow, contains a staircase leading to the lantern on top.

Trajan's Forum, the last of these public spaces to be built, covered an immense area 155 yards long and 95 yards wide. Entering through a huge archway, Trajan's subjects gazed across an expanse of snowy marble pavement at the tall statue of their emperor, mounted on horseback, in the center of the square. Beyond this heroic sculpture rose the multicolored marble columns of the new Basilica Ulpia, extending the full width of the forum. So vast were its spaces and manifold its uses that it has been described by one modern scholar as a "covered counterpart" of the forum itself. To the many provincial cities that copied it, the structure seemed to embody the essence of imperial Rome. Outside, the gilded bronze tiles of its gabled roof gleamed in the sun; on the inside, the colonnaded clerestory lit the sumptuous variety of marble veneers covering its walls and floor. At both ends of the nave were semicircular colonnaded apses. Beyond the basilica two libraries, one for books in each of the two languages of the empire—Latin and Greek—faced one another across a courtyard. Each enclosed two floors of rectangular niches that held about 40,000 scrolls. Between the libraries rose the great column of Trajan, with its spiral reliefs, which still stands. Just outside Trajan's Forum, the emperor constructed his great covered market, a complex of more than 150 individual stores and offices—rows of single room, two-story, barrel-vaulted shops—and a gabled hall five storys high.

The dramatic effect of Rome's architecture did not fade with time, even after the capital of the empire had shifted to Byzantium. In the spring of AD 357 the eastern emperor Constantius II arrived in Rome for a visit. The historian Ammianus recorded the ruler's reaction: "When he came into the Forum of Trajan, a construction in my view unique under the whole canopy of heaven, admired even by the unanimous verdict of the gods, then he stood still in amazement, turning his attention upon the vast complex around him, which is far beyond any description, and not again to be rivaled by mortal men. All hope of attempting anything like it was put aside."

The chronicler expressed no surprise that even the current emperor should be silenced by what he saw. For Trajan had finished what his predecessors had begun, by composing an unequivocal visual statement of grandeur, confidence, and unstoppable might. It had marked the moment when Rome was assured of her power, and it had provided a fitting stage for the drama of imperial glory that reached its climax under the emperor Hadrian.

SIC TRANSIT GLORIA

Now a place of mute stone, its silence impinged upon by the sounds of modern Rome pulsing endlessly around it, the Forum that was once the very heart of the ancient city's life reveals only here and there evidence of its former vitality. But a little imagination can bring it alive. Take postholes detected in the pavement by archaeologists; they once held supports for awnings used for special events, as when the Forum became a great dining room. Julius Caesar feasted the populace at 22,000 tables crowded into the Forum's marble confines. On another similarly grandiose occasion, a funeral for a respected citizen, tables had been set up without protective canopies. A sudden storm arose, with winds so forceful that the citizens had to spread the awnings. Tongues wagged that this was the punishment for the organizers' failure to follow the advice of the soothsayers who had urged them to go to the precaution of putting up tents.

Finds such as the postholes—or a gaming board scratched into the marble floor of the Basilica Julia—evoke the vitality of the Forum, long since reduced to a wilderness of crumbling monuments and rambling wisteria vines. But nothing puts flesh on its marble bones more vividly than history as spelled out in chronicles and revealed by scientists.

Here, through the ages of Roman greatness, people gathered to trade and deal, to vote and make laws, to honor or defame their leaders, and to supplicate their gods with earnest sacrifice. Here, in the Temple of Vesta (seen through the arch above) the vestal virgins carried on age-old rites. And here passions could often rule the day: Inflamed by fiery orators, mobs redressed unjust laws with violence and answered political outrage with murder. Not surprisingly, in the changing fortunes of this storied place—in the tales of natural disaster, of profligate growth, and of economic and political revolution written in its grand structures—historians have divined the fortunes of Rome itself.

REVISITING A HALLOWED MEETING PLACE

On any day of the week, just before dawn, Romans could be seen making their way to the Forum. Such pilgrimages were already a 600-year-old habit by the Augustan Age.

Specialty shoppers congregated on the upper Sacred Way, where women of wealth, accompanied by slaves, visited shops stocked with bolts of embroidered cloth and vials of scented oils. Those individuals with a taste for politics and oratory gathered near the Comitium at the Forum's western end. There, atop the dais known as the Rostra, magistrates held forth. Under the influence of the speakers' rhetoric, rival parties often fell to bloody scuffling, while, from nearby temples, nervous consuls intoned prayers and offered up animal sacrifices.

Milling about were vast, garrulous throngs, ever ready for a bit of gossip, a public execution, or a gladiatorial contest. By the rise of the empire, people, buildings, and monuments had so overwhelmed the ancient square that a series of new forums had to be built.

The remains of the Roman Forum (center) dominate this aerial photo. To the west (extreme left) lies the oldest section, comprising the senate house and Temple of Vesta. Later additions include the Basilica Nova (triple arches) and the Temple of Venus and Rome (far right). The imperial forums appear above and to the left.

IN THE HALLS OF POWER

En route to the senate house from their villas on the Palatine Hill, Roman senators had to cut a path through the Forum's throng. The legislators, conspicuous in their red shoes and white togas trimmed with purple, occasionally met with rude gibes and fisticuffs along the way. Even the senate house, the Curia, came in for its share of violence: In 52 BC, when Cicero defended the murderer of the gangster-tribune Clodius, an enraged mob tore the wooden benches from shops, piled them in the Curia, and—after laying Clodius' body inside—torched the whole lot.

The Curia did not languish in ruins for long. Widely esteemed, in Cicero's words, as "the shrine of wisdom and statesmanship, the very center of the city's life," it was promptly restored.

The nearby Tabularium, the national archives, weathered the vicissitudes of Roman politics better: Built in 78 BC, it survived nearly intact until the 1400s, when its second story was obliterated to erect the Palace of the Senator. What remains of the building—an arcade above a substructure 36 feet high and 11 feet thick—testifies to the importance once attached to its function. Here were stored all of Rome's official documents, as well as a portion of its wealth.

Divested of their ornamental facades, the Curia *(near building, right)* and the Tabularium *(hall with arches, left)* overlook the Arch of Severus and the ruins of the Basilica Julia. Erected on a rise, the government buildings dominated the open square where Roman crowds convened.*

Light spills through three arches into the Tabularium's lofty gallery. Originally, 10 such arches illuminated the arcade, but they were bricked up during the Dark Ages. The heaviness of the overlying palace precludes any possibility of reopening the remaining arches. Today the gallery is part of city hall.

A pattern of inlaid colored marble still graces the floor of the Curia, seen below as reconstructed by Diocletian after the great fire of AD 283. Marble steps to the left and right served as platforms for 300 senators' chairs. Presiding officials occupied the dais at the room's far end.

UNDER THE GAZE OF THE GODS

The venerated Temple of Castor and Pollux had more than a religious function. First dedicated in 484 BC to honor the divine warrior twins Castor and Pollux, the temple served not only as a site for military ceremonies and various pronouncements but also as a setting for certain senatorial functions. Its chambers, notes Cicero, were "daily thronged by those who come to consult on the gravest issues." The temple lay—somewhat incongruously—where Tuscan Street, with its traffic of filchers and prostitutes, met the ceremonial promenade of the Sacred Way.

Despite its sanctity, the temple was often the scene of raucous goings-on. Cicero relates how, in 65 BC, the consul Bibulus attempted to overpower his fellow consul, Julius Caesar, as he proclaimed the passage of a controversial law from the temple's podium. In response, Caesar's supporters splashed the unfortunate Bibulus with a bucket of excrement, then beat him up.

Far greater solemnity attended official Rome's relationship to the neighboring Temple of Vesta. The goddess of sacred fire, Vesta symbolized the perpetuity of Rome. Her flame, alight in the recesses of the shrine, was guarded by the six priestesses known as vestal virgins.

Though all traces of the original temple have vanished, votive pottery unearthed on the spot indicates that it was still in active use in 575 BC. The existing shrine dates from AD 200. Adjoining the temple was the House of the Vestals, where the priestesses resided in sumptuous comfort.

Awash in moonlight, the ruins of the Temples of Castor and Pollux (center) *and of Vesta* (left) *evince little of their former glory. Three columns recall the vast colonnade that once surrounded the former. In the court of the House of the Vestals* (inset), *statues of the priestesses rimmed a mirrorlike pool.*

Above all else, the Forum was the locus of Roman justice. In the early days of the republic, trials took place outdoors, on the pavement or on the porches of various temples. Loafers and idlers gathered around the proceedings—often pronouncing their own verdicts before the jury did.

By the second century BC the Romans had erected the first of the grand colonnaded halls, known as basilicas, that would become the Forum's centers for law and business interests. The most splendid, the Basilica Nova, was built in the fourth century AD. In its heyday, the hall—a cathedral-like edifice with a soaring nave illuminated by clerestory windows—bustled with lawyers, moneylenders, bankers, and merchants. In one of the building's two apses, set apart by a lofty balustrade, archaeologists have identified a court of law. A frieze of sea gods and nymphs once lent the court an imperial air, an effect enhanced by gilded walls and an inlaid marble floor.

Majestic even in decay, the Basilica Nova (triple arches, left) dominates the Forum's eastern end. Earthquakes have reduced the structure to one-third its original size. The surviving arches, each 80 feet high and 67 feet across, once formed part of the vaulted interior.

THE FORUMS OF THE CAESARS

Inevitably, as Rome grew ever bigger and the empire expanded, the old Forum proved too small. Caesar addressed the problem by creating the Forum Julium. The Roman chronicler Dio Cassius pronounced it "much more beautiful" than the well-used one. It was bounded on three sides by a portico of shops; at its center rose a temple of Venus, fronted by a babbling fountain.

Over the next 150 years, Rome's emperors would follow Caesar's lead in modeling their own imperial forums. Augustus' Forum, dedicated to the Roman god Mars, was home to Mars' warrior priests, who were renowned for their opulent banquets. The mouth-watering odors from one such fete seduced the emperor Claudius—at the time presiding over a tribunal—to adjourn court and hurry off to join the celebrants.

Rome's intelligentsia frequented the serene precinct of Vespasian's Forum. A cultural haven, it boasted formal gardens, a library, and a museum. To get there, Romans often traversed the narrow expanse of Nerva's Forum, which constituted a scenic corridor between the old forum and the new ones.

But the grandest of the forums would be the one bulit by Trajan. All of Rome flocked to the complex, a city unto itself. Here were the Basilica Ulpia and grand libraries of Greek and Latin flanking a gallery overlooking Trajan's Column—a 130-foot-high pillar carved with military reliefs. Shoppers thronged Trajan's market, a multistory arcade of 150 shops and warehouses not unlike a modern shopping mall.

A bird's-eye view reveals the relative location of three forums: At lower left is Caesar's; at lower right Augustus'; and at center the forum and semicircular market of Trajan. Obscuring Trajan's Column is scaffolding erected so the monument could be cleaned (left of center).

42

Shallow steps lead into recesses off the main portico of Augustus' Forum. In such semiprivate scholae, governors were invested before departing for the provinces, and civil suits were heard. Occasionally, scholae were the site of private religious ceremonies honoring Mars, the forum's patron deity.

Nestled against the Capitoline Hill, a ruined arcade yawns behind the colonnade bordering the Forum Julium. Shopkeepers once sold their wares from these dim recesses. Above the shops, an additional story provided apartments.

THE EMPEROR HADRIAN, CITIZEN OF THE WORLD

A lover of all things Greek, Emperor Hadrian wears the robe of a Greek philosopher in this statue showing his trademark beard and curls. The statue— one of many of the emperor found in the colonies—turned up in a temple of Apollo at Cyrene, in Libya.

The great princes and church-men of Renaissance Italy heightened the splendor of their urban palaces and countryseats with the ruins of imperial Rome that lay round about them. Statues of gods and emperors, busts of ancient heroes, stone nymphs that had danced on the rims of antique fountains were removed from sites where they had languished for 1,500 years, cleansed of the dust of ages, and, after bouts of bargaining between plunderers and purchasers, installed in magnificent residences of the rich and mighty.

So when Cardinal Ippolito d'Este built a villa in the district of Tivoli, in the mid-16th century, he employed his chief architect, Pirro Ligorio, to search a nearby piece of land for relics that would add luster to the palatial house and gardens. Rich pickings lay there, for the location that had charmed the cardinal had appealed, for much the same reasons, to a distinguished predecessor. Tivoli—with its deep gorge and its backdrop of hills, conveniently near Rome, and yet peacefully remote—had been the setting for the sumptuous residence of the emperor Hadrian.

The remains of the second-century AD sovereign's sprawling estate had once included perhaps as many as 300 acres of pleasure gardens, reception halls, banquet halls, baths, a library, porticoes, theaters, and an artificial island. There hundreds of ancient sculptures lay abandoned, hidden in silted up pools and under fallen stairs and more than a millennium's growth of unchallenged brambles.

In its heyday, the villa had housed not only Hadrian and the empress Sabina but also some of the senior officials who helped him run the empire. The estate may have been used by some of Hadrian's successors, but almost every emperor built his own luxurious villas. Busts of members of the Severan dynasty, AD 193-235, have been found there, the last evidence of imperial interest in the place. Over time, the estate fell into disrepair, prey to vandals and the elements, its purpose forgotten. Not until 1461, as scholars delved with fresh enthusiasm into the past, did Pope Pius II, together with Flavio Biondo, a student of ancient texts, make the connection between the architectural remains known as Old Tivoli and the imperial residence cited by a fourth-century writer.

Pirro Ligorio appreciated that the site held greater significance than its value as a repository of decorations for the cardinal's water gardens. In his own account of his work, he expressed his ambivalence about the task of procurement his patron had set him, "desiring with all my heart to revive and preserve the memory of ancient things, and at the same time to satisfy those who delight in them." Accordingly, he recorded what he saw, making a meticulous survey that included drawings of the villa's visible remains, before carting off statuary for His Eminence's pleasure.

The plunder continued for the next two centuries, as aristocrats from northern Europe toured Italy to look upon its ancient glories. They hungered for priceless works, and those associated with the illustrious Hadrian were especially desired. Eighteenth-century antiquarians made their fortunes and reputations by digging up sculptures at Tivoli and sending them off to embellish stately mansions and marbled town houses throughout Europe. Permits were required, however, and collectors often found themselves embroiled in litigation. There were also less acquisitive visitors. The German poet Goethe, braving the briars and scorpions in June 1787, noted in his journal that viewing the landscape at Tivoli was "one of those experiences that permanently enrich one's life."

Only in the 1870s did the first systematic excavation of Hadrian's Villa get underway. Archaeology began to be established on a scientific footing, and the Italian government had purchased about half the property from the heirs of an Italian noble. Notwithstanding their ruined state, the wonders that survive at Tivoli *(pages 69-79)*

patron's esteem and climbed the career ladder available to a man of his birth and abilities. He participated in major military campaigns in Central Europe and in the Near East, occupying posts on the emperor's staff and presiding as governor of Lower Pannonia—today, part of Hungary—on the empire's strategic northern border, the Danube River. Defending his territory against raids by Sarmatian tribesmen was not his only preoccupation. His successful battles against corruption by local officials demanded much of his attention and won him considerable prestige in Rome. At the age of 33, he gained promotion to the consulship, Rome's highest official honor. Nine years later, as Trajan lay on his deathbed, he allegedly adopted Hadrian and named him heir. Subsequently, gossip held that Plotina had forged the adoption papers, even delaying news of her husband's death until Hadrian received them.

In August 117 Hadrian became emperor of Rome. Some 1,800 years later, scholars who were studying an Egyptian papyrus dating from the era when the ancient Nile kingdom lay under Roman rule found documentary evidence of some of the festivities marking the new ruler's accession. The text records part of a dramatic presentation, performed in an Egyptian town, to commemorate the great event. An actor, who represented the sun god Phoebus Apollo, formally delivered the news of the old emperor's deification and the arrival of his successor: "I have just risen on high with Trajan in my white-horsed chariot. I come to you people to proclaim Hadrian as the new ruler, whom all things gladly serve for his ability and the genius of his Divine Father."

This new emperor had not, in his youth, inspired awe among the crusty senators of the imperial capital. Once, while delivering an official address in the Senate, on Trajan's behalf, he was derided for his provincial accent. During this same period, he was regarded as a dangerous flouter of convention among the clean-shaven patricians for affecting a beard. On surviving portrait busts and coins, he sports

A tight-lipped Sabina, wife of Hadrian, reveals none of her secrets in this marble bust. While Hadrian cared little for Sabina, he always insisted that she be treated with the dignity worthy of an empress. She eventually came to hate him.

49

a close-cut beard, setting a fashion future emperors would follow. His intention was to identify himself with the bearded philosophers of ancient Greece. In this he may have been advised by Polemo, a distinguished philosopher, and others of his *amici,* the circle of close friends with whom an emperor discussed policy and cultural matters.

Strong and well-built, Hadrian was taller than average and elegant in his dress and demeanor. During his military career, he subjected himself to the same physical exertions and deprivations his troops endured. He would swim in the bone-chilling Danube when conditions demanded it and share the rough rations in the field, in spite of his reputation as something of a gourmet (a "right good eater of rich food," according to one of his contemporaries). In his leisure time, Hadrian was an energetic rider and hunter. During a sojourn in southern France, he erected a monument to the memory of a beloved hunting horse, Borysthenes, writing a poetic epitaph: "Caesar's hunter, over plain and marsh, and the mounds of Tuscany, went like the wind. After the boars of Hungary, he chased, and no boar dared wound him." This tribute was not his only literary effort. He wrote speeches, opinions, a book of sayings, and an autobiography—all of it, except a few lines, now lost—and tried his hand at poetry, including verses dedicated to the god of love.

Hadrian felt at home with the arts. His intellectual abilities impressed his biographers sufficiently to cause at least one to claim he was capable of dictating memoranda, writing literary compositions, listening to reports by underlings, and making brilliant conversation with friends—all at the same time. A less dazzled chronicler called him a "versatile dilettante." He sang, played the flute, discussed the fine points of painting, architecture, and mathematics with dinner companions, and expressed a preference for the earlier authors over such better-known later writers as Cicero and Virgil.

The emperor's enthusiasm was fiercest for the ancient civilization of Greece. Like most educated Romans, although more intensely, he regarded the Hellenic past as the wellspring of high culture. Its literature, architecture, philosophy, and sculpture provided models that Romans would do well to imitate. People who knew him well called him Graeculus, or Little Greek.

Hadrian could be volatile and unpredictable. It was whispered that he posted spies to keep even his friends and allies under surveillance and was quick to take offense. Intimates fallen out of favor could find themselves suddenly barred from his presence or banished altogether from Rome. But he was also capable of compassion. When a deranged slave lunged at him with murder in mind, for instance, he insisted that the would-be assassin should not be harmed but placed in the care of physicians.

A collection of 13 of Hadrian's administrative decisions have survived under the title *Remarks;* they show something of his style as a ruler. One incident concerned an appeal by a man whose sons were conscripted for military service. They were, he explained, ignorant and feckless youths, and he dreaded to think what might happen if they stepped out of line and got into trouble. Hadrian tried to reassure the man that his boys were only going off for peacetime duty and that his fears were groundless. But the petitioner beseeched Hadrian, "Oh please, Lord Emperor, send me instead, or let me go as their servant so that I can look after them." This seemed an abhorrent notion to Hadrian, who perhaps was influenced by Roman law, where the father once held the power of life and death over his children and still was a figure to be reckoned with in his family. "God forbid that I should send you to wait on your children," Hadrian said. Instead he bestowed upon the man the rank of centurion and put him in charge of the troops to which his sons had been assigned.

On another occasion, Hadrian, as a mark of his favor, was distributing bonuses to a group of soldiers. A ragged woman, watching from the sidelines, suddenly called out, "Lord Emperor, please tell them to give me an allotment from my son's share! He neglects me, he does!" The soldier in question angrily cut in: "I don't recognize this woman as my mother!" To which Hadrian replied, "In that case, I don't recognize you as a Roman citizen."

Hadrian's sense of responsibility for his people and his accessibility to them is summed up in the story of the woman who pushed a petition in his direction as he was walking along the street. Seeing that he ignored her, she shouted, "then cease being emperor!" Hearing this, he turned back and dealt with her case.

But the emperor's humane dispensing of justice did not mean he was easily manipulated. A man once came to see him with a sad tale about a miscarriage of justice: His aged father had been fined, wrongly, for some offense and had had much of his property confiscated. The son wanted the case reopened. Hadrian asked when the incident had taken place. When told, "Ten years ago, my lord," he could hardly contain his irritation, as he turned down the appeal. "Well, why didn't you go and see the prefect and put your case to him before? It's all your own fault. If we are going to dig up and retry old decisions, whether right or wrong, we'll be at it forever."

Legal and judicial reform was a subject close to Hadrian's heart. To cut through the tangle of old and often contradictory laws and edicts, he recruited an African jurist and civil servant named Salvius Julianus to create a straightforward legal code. The task took nearly 10 years, but when it was finished, the empire boasted a more efficient legal apparatus, one that would remain in place long after Rome itself had fallen.

Among the many changes Hadrian introduced were new laws improving the treatment of slaves. No longer would Roman citizens be entitled to kill or castrate their slaves or punish them by shipping them off to brothels or gladiatorial academies. Henceforward, slaves would have to be sentenced before a court. He ended the practice of automatically executing all slaves in a household where one of their number had murdered the master and abolished the forced-labor camps to which slaves and freemen alike had previously been sentenced. He did not, however, put a stop to the time-honored insistence on extracting testimony from slave witnesses by torture, although he attacked the practice as untrustworthy and dangerous.

Still, no slave could become too complacent. One of his biographers relates Hadrian's displeasure at the sight of a slave attached to the imperial household—probably a highly educated government clerk—speaking on familiar terms to two visiting senators and walking off with them as if he were their social equal. Hadrian promptly ordered another slave to hurry after the trio and give the offender a salutary smack on the ear, to remind him who he was. Yet, the emperor had less regard than many aristocrats for class distinctions and counted among his friends Epictetus, a stoic philosopher who had been born a slave.

Slaves and senators alike benefited from Hadrian's improvements in running the city and the empire as a whole. Even modest changes—such as banning heavily laden wagons and riders on horseback from Rome's narrow streets—produced an appreciable and immediate upgrading of the quality of life in the capital. More subtle, but far reaching, was Hadrian's new-broom approach to government, some of which had become corrupt. Paid informers and cartels of bribe-taking officials were swept out. Instead, the emperor appointed and promoted public servants, increasingly on merit rather than solely on family connections. Like Hadrian himself, many had

provincial backgrounds, for he recruited the best people from Gaul, Africa, Dalmatia, Greece, Egypt, and other parts of the empire. They were assigned to important divisions of government, where hierarchies of chief secretaries and staff supervised areas ranging from state finance to official correspondence and the purchasing of supplies.

To help the civil service, Hadrian also reformed the postal network—a system of relay riders and vehicles that carried urgent communications and imperial dignitaries over the network of roads stretching across the empire, mostly built by the soldiers. Previously the maintenance of the system was the responsibility of the commu-

Few of the 55-foot-tall columns remain of Athens' massive 135-by-354-foot temple to Zeus, which was completed by Hadrian in 131-132 and marked the center of his new city. Grateful Athenians flattered the emperor with the title "Olympian."

nities along its routes. But Hadrian, recognizing that good communications were essential to maintaining the empire, acknowledged that the imperial treasury should take responsibility for the system.

Rome was the seat of imperial power, but Hadrian felt no obligation to remain there. In 121 he turned his face and footsteps abroad. Some of his predecessors had, when necessary, bestirred themselves from Italy for the purposes of conquest and pacification. But none had absented himself for so long. Hadrian's journeys fulfilled his vision of a ruler's duty. He traveled not only for military reasons but also to see for himself the circumstances throughout the empire. He wanted to be a visible presence among the people, to judge and build, and constantly to improve. He also had an insatiable desire to know everything.

When Hadrian entered Athens—center of the old Hellenic world to which he was so passionately devoted—he was in his spiritual home. He visited the city four or five times as emperor, prolonging each stay and enrolling himself officially as an Athenian citizen. Even before Hadrian had become emperor, in 112, the Athenians had elected him archon, or chief magistrate, a great honor. Inspired by the

In this tomb painting from Rome's port of Ostia, porters load grain onto a small merchant ship, the Isis Giminiana, *for transportation upriver to the capital. The captain, Farnaces, is at the rudder and beside him stands Abascantus, most likely the vessel's owner. The porter in the bow says, "Feci" (Done), indicating that he has completed his task.*

city's history and ruined glories, he launched scores of ambitious schemes for its embellishment. The inhabitants of other provincial capitals had been dazzled by his beneficence, but these projects paled before his Athenian endeavors. He could not do enough for Athens.

When the dust cleared from the construction sites, Athenians found themselves with a massive gymnasium flanked by 100 pillars of imported Libyan stone, a magnificent library, and a completely new city quarter. The boundary between the old city and the new district was marked by a monumental, two-story arch, about 20 feet wide, which probably framed statues of the ancient Athenian hero and founder of Athens, Theseus, and one of Hadrian himself. "This is Athens, the ancient city of Theseus," announces an inscription on the side of the portal facing the Roman Forum. "This is the city of Hadrian, and not of Theseus," replies the carved declaration on the other side. The gate and its writing remain to this day.

Inside the new quarter lay an architectural wonder, the Olympieion, a great temple to the Olympian Zeus, which had been started in 174 BC on the site of an ancient shrine but remained unfinished until Hadrian's energy completed it. Four statues of Hadrian—two made of granite ferried all the way from Egypt—greeted the visitors to the shrine. The structure rose to the awe-inspiring height of 90 feet and boasted more than 100 columns. In its inner sanctum stood a colossal ivory and gold statue of Zeus. The result would certainly have been dramatic, but perhaps it was a trifle overblown for some aesthetic tastes. The second-century travel writer Pausanias, reporting on the glories of Greece, merely says it was "worth seeing," noting that "considering its size, the workmanship is good."

The completion of this venerable temple was not an isolated accomplishment. Wherever he went, Hadrian paid his respects to the local gods, not only visiting the principal shrines but restoring those that had decayed or—as in Athens—building new ones. Like his contemporaries, Hadrian was intrigued by the ancient religions of the eastern Mediterranean world. If all roads now led to Rome, it was only fitting that the old deities of Egypt and Asia, such as Osiris, Mithra, and Isis, should find their way there, where the diverse civilizations of the empire met and mingled. His peregrinations offered him an unparalleled opportunity to explore the ancient cults firsthand, sometimes with intellectual detachment, sometimes with the passion of a pilgrim.

During an earlier stay in Greece, probably before he became emperor, Hadrian had become an initiate into the mystery cult of the earth goddess Demeter at Eleusis, near Athens. The shrine stood on the very spot where—according to myth—Demeter's daughter, Persephone, was released after her abduction by Hades, king of the underworld. Demeter had convinced Hades to allow his reluctant bride an annual visit to the land of the living. Based on this metaphor, the Eleusinian mysteries promised renewal and a better life.

Together with a throng of devotees from all walks of life, Hadrian began the lengthy process of this initiation with formal instruction in the tenets of the cult. This was followed by communal purgings in the sea, then a long march from Athens over the hills to the sacred shrine, accompanied by chants and ritual mockery by masked onlookers, religious dramas by torchlight, and prescribed rounds of drinking, fasting, and sacrifice. Finally, a mounting wave of communal exultation culminated in a secret ceremony held in a darkened temple. A high priest, who appeared in a blaze of light, conducted this ritual with a display of sacred objects. He then metaphorically led the spellbound supplicants to the edge of death and helped them leap across the chasm to immortality.

Thousands of people took part in these ceremonies, and most of them must have adhered to the command that the details of the ritual climax be kept secret, for no precise description of the events has ever been found. But the historian Plutarch, also an initiate, recorded his own responses: "Just before the end, the terror is at its worst. There is shivering, trembling, cold sweat, and fear. But the eyes perceive a wonderful light. Purer regions are reached and fields where there is singing and dancing, and sacred words and divine visions inspire a holy awe."

Hadrian's emotions must have been similar to those of Plutarch. Thirsting for even greater wisdom, he sought a higher grade of initiation, available only to a small and dedicated elite of devotees, at the hands of a priestess of the shrine. There is no information on whether this occurred before or after he became emperor, for the evidence of the encounter comes from the writings of Hadrian's spiritual instructress, whose encomium on her celebrated pupil has survived: "The master of the vast earth and the sterile sea, the sovereign of innumerable mortals, Hadrian, who has poured out indescribable riches on all the cities."

Revisiting as emperor the scene of his earlier spiritual renewal, Hadrian had his appetite for hidden knowledge whetted once more. Before long he was to be found in one of the old priestly sanctuaries of Egypt, the half-abandoned city of Heliopolis, studying magical incantations, the setting of curses, and the invocation of spirits under a scholarly priest named Pancrates. Some tutorials took place in the recesses of the sun god's temple; some—to Hadrian's amazement—took place in the emperor's own dreams, where Pancrates appeared and—in the words of a surviving priestly papyrus—"proved the complete truth of his magic." To express his admiration for his teacher's gifts, Hadrian "ordered that he be given a double remuneration."

Elsewhere in Egypt, Hadrian studied astrology, a preoccupation of many ancient scholars. According to his biographers, he proved a talented pupil, learning to cast a horoscope as accurately as

HIGH LIVING IN ANCIENT TIMES

Since the third century BC, Rome's builders had been erecting high-rise apartment dwellings called insulae to house the city's burgeoning population. Three, four, and sometimes five stories high, these timber-framed tenements were often poorly constructed, and fire was a constant danger: "If the alarm goes at ground level," wrote the first-century AD satirist Juvenal, "the last to fry will be the attic tenant." Indeed, after the disastrous Great Fire of AD 64 the emperor Nero tried to regulate construction, imposing a 70-foot limit on the height of insulae and a 10-foot space between buildings. Although they once housed much of Rome's citizenry—there were 25 insulae to every private dwelling by the end of the empire—few traces of these apartment blocks remain in the capital. The best-preserved ruins are found farther on down the Tiber, at the port of Ostia, with some dating from Hadrian's reign.

Built of brick-faced concrete, the tall apartment blocks of Ostia ranged along the town's broad, straight streets, their abundant windows facing out above tiers of jutting balconies. Storefronts with barrel-vaulted ceilings typically occupied the ground-floor level, interspersed with stone staircases that led to the upper stories. While rooms were often spacious, amenities were limited: Apartments lacked cooking facilities and only those on the ground floor had lavatories. But many of the insulae could boast a central courtyard, which provided light and ventilation for inner rooms and a cistern supplying water for upper stories. The largest blocks in Ostia accommodated more than 100 tenants, and some may have sheltered as many as 300.

This view of Ostia's main street, the Decamus Maximus, shows remains of the insulae for which the port is famous. One apartment block is reconstructed in model form above. Fancier buildings featured windows of glass, mica, or transparent gypsum; the plainer ones had oiled paper or shutters.

any official astrologer could have done. In fact, he was said to have drawn up a chart that correctly foretold the hour of his own death.

Back home in Italy, Hadrian's subjects were less convinced of his devotion to their interests. His relationship with the citizens of the imperial capital was fraught with difficulties. Those whom he had removed from office for corruption or incompetence slandered him. Others suspected that his true allegiance was to Athens, rather than Rome. Perhaps in compensation, Hadrian launched into a program of municipal improvements, restoration works, and imposing new buildings within the capital and its environs.

One major public-works project was Hadrian's development of Rome's seaport satellite, Ostia, lying 20 miles away, at the mouth of the Tiber River. Trajan had built a new artificial harbor to receive the flood of imported wine, wheat, and other goods arriving from Roman colonies around the Mediterranean rim. As the port prospered, Ostia became something of a boom town. Following Trajan's lead, Hadrian carried out a massive building project to transform what had once been a modest coastal community into a densely packed city of some 30,000 souls.

Systematic excavations began in Ostia in the early part of the 20th century, under the direction of two Italians, Dante Vaglieri and Guido Calza. Their discoveries reveal much about how people lived there in Hadrian's day. As in Rome itself, space was at a premium. A partial solution, then as now, was to extend upwards, replacing small individual dwelling houses with large apartment blocks rising three to five storys high. These imposing structures—called insulae, literally "islands"—were built of fireproof concrete faced with bricks. Small shops or factories with sleeping room usually occupied the ground levels, often incorporating mezzanines that provided additional living accommodations. Above them, stacked one above the other, were self-contained apartments, some with many rooms, linked by two to five stairways to the street. Architectural models, based on the early digs, suggest that these buildings would not look out of place in a modern Italian city.

Within the capital itself, Hadrian attended to repair, long overdue, in the more-than-a-century-old Forum of Augustus and on the Palatine Hill. He created landmarks that changed the face of the Eternal City: among them was the Temple of Venus and Rome, which he designed and which was larger in size than any religious building Rome had yet seen. He also built a temple dedicated to his predecessor, the recently deified Trajan. Over the Tiber, he constructed a new bridge; its three central arches still support the modern Pons Aelius, which preserves as well Hadrian's family name. At the end of this bridge, Hadrian erected a massive rotunda of concrete sheathed in stone (completed after his death by his successor Antoninus Pius) to house his remains and the remains of those who would follow him to the throne. As the papal fortress, Castel Sant'Angelo, the structure still dominates the riverbank. Alaric's Visigoths looted the urns containing the ashes of Hadrian and Sabina along with most of the building's other contents when they sacked Rome in 410. Its statues were flung from the ramparts upon the attacking Goths in 537, to little avail. Over the centuries the building's marble facing was stripped; it was probably burned, as so much ancient marble has been over time, to make lime for mortar.

The Pantheon *(pages 61-63),* the great domed rotunda dedicated to the empire's gods, still standing in its entirety, was another of Hadrian's structures. The immensity of scale, the circular shape, the high-vaulted dome expressed Hadrian's aspirations for the em-

Across the statue lined Pons Aelius—three arches of which belong to Hadrian's original bridge—looms the huge stone drum of Rome's formidable Castel Sant'Angelo, the mausoleum built by Hadrian. In ancient times the drum's upper portion was faced with marble and boasted a roof garden; today the structure houses a military museum.

pire—self-contained, eternal, situated at the heart of the cosmos, and enclosed by the high vault of the heavens. The ideas expressed in the designs of the Pantheon and other structures he built reflect Hadrian's own, for he took a lively interest in architectural matters, even consulting Apollodorus, the most celebrated architect of the age.

The earliest recorded encounter between the pair was not a happy one. According to the historian Dio Cassius' account, they first locked horns during Trajan's reign. Hadrian, standing by while his imperial cousin and Apollodorus consulted on some work under construction, interrupted their conversation with a bit of criticism. Busy and blunt, Apollodorus dismissed Hadrian's contribution to the discussion with the gibe, "Be off, and draw your pumpkins. You don't understand any of these matters." Scholars speculate that there may be a connection between the "pumpkins" Hadrian was drawing and three domes, often called gourd domes, that ornament three different buildings still standing at Hadrian's Villa.

Yet many years later, when Hadrian, as emperor, began the construction of his great Temple of Venus and Rome for the capital, he sent the design to Apollodorus for comment. Dio, not always the most sympathetic of chroniclers where Hadrian was concerned, suggested that the emperor's intention was to show off his own architectural genius to Apollodorus. When he received the plans, Apollodorus was not impressed. He replied that the setting for the shrine was wrong; it was far too low and inconspicuous. Instead the main floor of the temple should be erected upon chambers constructed at the lower levels, to allow the building to occupy a commanding position over the Sacred Way. The resulting basement space would then make convenient storerooms for the equipment used in the Flavian Amphitheater next door. And indoors, why such a low ceiling? The statues of goddesses that had been sculpted for the interior walls were much too tall for the space allowed them. "If the goddesses wanted to get up and go out, they would hit their heads on the ceiling," he allegedly said.

The archaeological evidence suggests that the emperor may have taken Apollodorus' criticisms to heart, for the temple's remains occupy the top of a lofty terrace that contains rooms adjacent to the amphitheater. When Hadrian was ready to begin this enormous enterprise in 121, he first had to move a colossal statue of Nero, 99 feet tall, from the site he had chosen for his new temple to another spot. The relocation required the efforts of 24 elephants pulling the upright figure on a platform—possibly on wheels or skids.

Hadrian was receptive to new design ideas and eager to put them into practice. And nowhere did he translate these architectural passions into bricks and mortar so freely and creatively as in his villa at Tivoli. Among its many dramatic experiments in landscape architecture is a section usually called the Canopus, a name also applied to the western mouth of the Nile. Some observers see the area as evocative of the Nile Delta, complete with a canal, a massive hillside grotto, and a stone statue of a crocodile. A few scholars have suggested that this site hints poignantly at a traumatic episode in Hadrian's private life, when the person he loved most—or, as some would have it, the only one he ever truly loved—drowned in the Nile.

Marriage and romantic love were not, in the Roman psyche, inextricably entangled. In 100, when the young Hadrian had exchanged the customary betrothal rings and nuptial vows with the 12- or 14-year-old Sabina, great-niece of the emperor Trajan, he probably did so not out of passion but for the reasons many ambitious young men chose wives. Weddings cemented family alliances, worked to the economic and social advantage of the contracting parties and their kin, and established a lawful context for the production of heirs. Mutual and lasting affection often developed, if the epitaphs of grieving Roman widows and widowers are to be believed. But this did not occur, according to the chroniclers, in the case of Hadrian and his young bride.

There seems to have been little love lost between Hadrian and Sabina and a great deal of conjecture about their relationship. Hadrian is said to have called his wife "moody and difficult" and lamented the fact that, because of his status, he could not easily divorce her out of hand, as a private citizen might have done. Childless marriages had become increasingly common among upper-class Romans during this period, and Hadrian was the third emperor in succession to produce no legitimate heir. Sabina is reported to have declared that she had made certain—by some contraceptive method never specified—that she would never bear a child by Hadrian. At least one historian asserts that it was Hadrian, not his wife, who ensured that the match would remain barren. For the imperial couple's incompatibility may have had more to do with Hadrian's apparent preference for his own sex. In the classical Mediterranean world, male homosexual love was not automatically stigmatized. Greek poets extolled it, and in Rome only those men who consist-

HADRIAN'S MASTERPIECE: THE PANTHEON, TEMPLE TO HONOR ALL THE GODS

Erected by Hadrian—and perhaps even designed by him—as a temple of all the gods, the Pantheon remains one of the grandest monuments of ancient Rome. As shown by dates stamped on its bricks, it was constructed sometime between AD 118 and 128 and replaced an earlier temple built on the same site by Augustus' minister and son-in-law, Marcus Agrippa, in 27 BC. Hadrian's Pantheon, however, was to be a more ambitious affair. In fact, Agrippa's temple would almost have fitted inside the new building, a daring domed rotunda fronted by a pedimental porch.

Raised up on a flight of five steps now partially buried, the Pantheon's huge colonnaded facade almost obscured the rest of the structure. The portico's 16 Corinthian columns, arranged in three rows, are immense: Each of the granite shafts measures 41 feet in height and almost 5 feet in diameter and weighs around 60 tons. And while the temple front is impressive, the combination of a conventional rectangular porch with a domed cylinder strikes some viewers as disharmonious. The temple's true grandeur lies beyond—for the Pantheon invites examination from within as well as without.

Through a bronze door mounted on a sill of green African marble is the great hall, a vast roofed rotunda, its diameter the same as its height. Reinforced by a web of stress-relieving arches embedded in the walls, the structure sits on a foundation of ringed concrete 24 feet wide and 15 feet deep, from which rise eight spoke-like concrete piers that flank the temple's entranceway and seven great niches.

The crowning glory of the Pantheon, however, is its vast vaulted ceiling, which rises boldly to the oculus, an eyelike opening. Molded into the concrete dome's inner surface are 140 coffers, arranged in five horizontal rows of 28 coffers each, which diminish in size toward the top. Once they held gilded-bronze rosettes. The significance of these panels was not purely ornamental, however, since they also significantly reduce the weight of the roof. Weight considerations also determined the quantity and types of materials used. As the dome curves toward its apex, its concrete mass—estimated at around 5,000 tons—shrinks progressively, from a width of 20 feet at its base to just 5 feet at the oculus. While the lower portions of the dome are made of concrete containing brick

Behind a cross-topped obelisk from the 18th century rise the portico and dome of the Pantheon in this partial view of the facade. Hadrian had the name of the builder of the temple that had originally stood on the site, Marcus Agrippa, inscribed on the pediment of the new structure.

and stone, volcanic pumice was used to lighten the heaviness of the uppermost zone.

Medieval myth held that this giant dome was built over a great mound of dirt piled up within the drum. To make sure that it was removed speedily after the dome was finished, Hadrian supposedly sprinkled gold pieces throughout the earth. The actual building technique—pouring successive rings of concrete against a coffered wooden mold—was no less ingenious.

At the top of the dome, through the broad oculus, light continues to flood into the windowless hall, bathing the interior in a gentle illumination.

Rains find their way inside in the same way, falling to the slightly crowned marble floor that diverts the water into drainage channels around the floor's edges.

A triumphant achievement, the Pantheon is a much-copied, but never equaled, structure. Although repaired many times— and long stripped of its bronze roof tiles—the temple preserves its majesty. In 609 the emperor Phocas presented the building to

Pope Boniface IV, who transformed it into a church, the Holy Mary of the Martyrs. Over the years various towers were added to the porch. But the simple and satisfying proportions of the great domed temple could not be improved upon, and the later additions were finally removed.

Today the Panethon is a national shrine as well as a church, a suitable place for the tombs of two Italian kings and a Renaissance master, the painter Raphael. Even so, the Pantheon remains substantially as it was in Hadrian's day and endures as one of the most complete and satisfying buildings of the classical world.

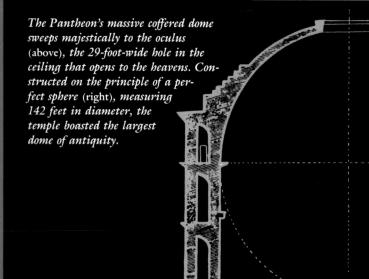

The Pantheon's massive coffered dome sweeps majestically to the oculus (above), *the 29-foot-wide hole in the ceiling that opens to the heavens. Constructed on the principle of a perfect sphere* (right), *measuring 142 feet in diameter, the temple boasted the largest dome of antiquity.*

A shaft of sunlight streams into the Pantheon's otherwise unlit interior through the oculus in the ceiling, an opening that doubtlessly symbolized the all-seeing eye of heaven. The building is an exemplary statement of Hadrian's world, ideated and symbolized—earth, sky, cosmos, empire—with all the Greco-Roman gods looking benevolently on Rome.

ently took the passive, supposedly "feminine" role were subjected to derision. A handsome youth, whether slave or patrician, might be a legitimate object for an older man's affections.

But few passions for an attractive young man could have caused the reverberations of Hadrian's relationship with a boy called Antinoüs, from the province of Bithynia in northwestern Asia Minor. His appearance is well-known, through more than 500 surviving portrait busts, heads, statues, and reliefs, created in response to the emperor's devotion. They memorialize a handsome, well-built, curly-headed youth, with deep-set almond eyes, high cheekbones, and a sensuous mouth. "You, with the face that is full of grace" sang a musician in his honor. The countenance would also fascinate future generations. In the 19th century, the English poet Alfred, Lord Tennyson, strolling among the Roman sculptures in the British Museum, paused before Antinoüs' bust and declared, "Ah—this is the inscrutable Bithynian. If we knew what he knew, we should understand the ancient world."

Whatever else his knowledge, it is surmised that the Bithynian knew how to spellbind an emperor. He may have encountered Hadrian during the emperor's travels in Asia Minor, and perhaps Hadrian sent Antinoüs to Rome to complete his education. Some historians speculate that he was a pupil at the training school for imperial pages on the Caelian Hill, where, at the hands of a formidable contingent of freed slaves, the spoiled sons of the provincial upper classes were transformed into fledgling courtiers. By the time he was 18 years of age, he may have become part of the ruler's inner circle.

Sculpted hunting scenes on the Arch of Constantine in Rome, conceived if not completed during Hadrian's reign, provide evidence of Antinoüs' rise. In one medallion, we see him taking part in a wild-boar hunt, riding alongside a senior member of the court and positioned just behind Hadrian. In another scene, he appears somewhat older and shorn of his adolescent curls, standing side by side with the emperor over the body of a fallen lion, killed during a celebrated hunt in the Libyan desert in 130.

Almost 18 centuries later, in 1910, an account of this adventure turned up on a papyrus found crumpled up inside an ancient clay vessel near the Nile. The text proved to be a partly decipherable epic, written by an Alexandrian poet, commemorating the same lion hunt

In a medallion adorning the Arch of Constantine, Hadrian (second from the left) *and his beloved Antinoüs* (far left) *each place a triumphant foot on the mane of the enormous lion that the emperor slew in the Libyan desert.*

shown on the arch in Rome. The quarry was a dreaded man-eater, and it had been an exciting chase: "Hadrian was the first to hurl his brass-fitted spear; he wounded the beast but did not kill it, for he intended to miss the mark, wishing to test to the full the sureness of aim of the beautiful Antinoüs." There followed some harrowing moments, as the beast hurled himself at his pursuers. The manuscript becomes illegible as the plot thickens, but the triumphant conclusion is decipherable: Just as the lion charges at Antinoüs, Hadrian intervenes to deliver the deathblow "with his own hand."

For perhaps three years, Antinoüs was a fixture in Hadrian's entourage, which also included Sabina. Artists were kept busy creating images of the imperial favorite. At least seven sculptures of Antinoüs have been found at the villa, where only two of the empress Sabina have so far come to light. When the emperor set off for Athens late in 128 and traveled through the east, making public appearances and investigating mystical rites, Antinoüs was with him for at least part of the trip.

The days of their companionship did not last forever. In 130, not long after the famous lion hunt, the imperial entourage cruised along the Nile to the ancient Egyptian capital of Thebes. Few details are known of the sudden tragedy that occurred along the way. At a village of rough mud huts called Hir-Wer, peasants lifted the corpse of the drowned Antinoüs from the river. Hadrian, in a fragment of autobiography preserved by Dio Cassius, would say no more than "he fell into the Nile." It may have been a simple accident, but biographers writing from the safe distance of several generations expressed suspicion. Suggestions ranged from foul play at the hands of rivals to a voluntary sacrifice on the part of the youth himself. For instance, some proposed that Antinoüs might have drowned himself for the noble purpose of enhancing Hadrian's sway over Egypt. In this version, he was placating the river gods, who had for two years diminished the all-important flooding of the Nile.

In his grief, Hadrian encouraged the deification of his lost companion. As a memorial, the emperor founded a city called Antinoopolis, sacred to the Bithynian's memory, on the site of Hir-Wer, overlooking that part of the Nile where he had died. Even the skies offered a monument, for shortly after the tragedy, Hadrian's astronomers observed a hitherto undiscovered heavenly body, located be-

A second Hadrianic roundel from the arch shows the mounted emperor hunting a wild boar. The curly-headed Antinoüs (middle) also rides in pursuit of the beast. The panels, dating from Hadrian's reign, were incorporated into the arch by Constantine 177 years after his predecessor's death in AD 138.

tween the Eagle and the Zodiac. They assured the emperor that this was the soul of Antinoüs, glowing with eternal life. The star they found still bears his name.

The cult of Antinoüs spread rapidly through Hadrian's dominions. Different parts of the empire worshiped him in ways reflecting their own cultural diversity. Egyptians associated Antinoüs with Osiris, who died in the Nile and was resurrected, bringing new life and fecundity to the land; Greeks and Romans most commonly portrayed him as a version of Dionysus, another reborn fertility god. Within 10 years of his death, Antinoüs was worshiped in at least 40 cities of the eastern empire, with new priesthoods, cultic shrines, or memorial games and festivals. Between 133 and 137, some 30 Greek cities minted coins and medallions in his honor. In Italy, Greece, Asia Minor, and the Near East, sculptors' workshops reverberated with the sounds of artisans, turning out hundreds of bronze and marble statues of Antinoüs.

Wherever Rome held sway, the deified Bithynian found worshipers. The rich adorned themselves with jewels incised with his features. Balkan miners sought the new god's blessing in a specially built temple before they faced the dangers of their subterranean workplaces; in the Italian town of Lanuvium a burial society formed, with the goddess Diana and Antinoüs as celestial patrons. Deep in the Caucasus, worshipers venerated a statue of Antinoüs in a mountain shrine.

The image of the emperor's beloved traveled farther than its human prototype ever had,

In this colossal polished-granite statue of Hadrian's favorite, Antinoüs appears as a god of Egypt, the land where he perished under mysterious circumstances in AD 130. Some 500 likenesses of Antinoüs survive into modern times, double the number of portraits of Hadrian himself.

even with the peripatetic Hadrian. Archaeologists excavating sites in Holland, the Rhineland, and along the Danube have unearthed quantities of bronze incense jars decorated with a crude copy of the famous face. Even in distant Britain, Antinoüs must have been known: An early 20th-century Englishman, out for a winter walk near Godmanchester, unearthed a coin bearing the sacred likeness.

One mystery, however, still piques archaeologists. The tomb of Antinoüs remains to be found. Exploring the ruins of Antinoopolis in the late 19th century, the French archaeologist Albert Gayet discovered 500,000 jars containing the offerings of pilgrims belonging to the Antinoüs cult. He mused upon the possibility of a tomb not far away, "in some lost corner of the mountains" from which "his body, embalmed with care, could one day be rendered back to us. What a revelation for the scholarly world would be this reappearance of a face so familiar!" In Rome, a badly damaged and almost indecipherable inscription on an obelisk was reinterpreted in 1975. The mysterious writing is missing keywords and is written in oddly constructed Egyptian hieroglyphs, and the recent translation, still disputed by scholars, reads: "O, Antinoüs! This deceased one, who rests in this tomb in the country estate of the Emperor of Rome."

In 1952 archaeologists at Tivoli began to excavate the section of the villa known as the Canopus. From the depths of the old waterway they lifted parts of arches and lengths of stone. Some scholars speculate that these might have been the supports for a stone roof or canopy. Statues found there include four Grecian maidens—copies of the caryatids from the Erechtheum on the Acropolis of Athens—and two giant satyrs holding baskets of fruit. These images were familiar features in the funeral architecture of Hadrian's age, appearing often as the props for canopies over tombs. But if Antinoüs rests at the villa, he remains, so far, undisturbed.

With or without the remains of his friend, Hadrian returned to Tivoli. He spent the remaining years of life largely among its landscapes and pavilions, perhaps contemplating the villa's ever-growing collection of Antinoüs images, produced, at his behest, by leading artists of his day. Despite suffering from what some scholars think was a painful form of arteriosclerosis, he continued with the business of government. To ensure that his own version of the reign would endure, he dictated his autobiography, which survived long enough to provide this necessary fodder for his third- and fourth-century biographers. In time for the 20th anniversary of his reign, he issued a series of coins, to be circulated throughout Rome's vast domains, commemorating his visits to the provinces.

One task remained—the naming of an heir to the throne. Hadrian designated as his successor a young patrician named Commodus, who now renamed himself Lucius Aelius Caesar. The young man was not regarded with great enthusiasm by his prospective subjects. His tastes, it was said, ran to Persian perfumes, beds filled with rose petals, and pageboys wearing gauzy wings. In accordance with his social position he had a wife, who protested against his extramarital dalliances. In response, he told her, "To be a wife is a duty, not a pleasure." He died of an illness before ever tasting power.

Hadrian soon announced a more cautious choice for the succession—a level-headed senator who would reign under the name of Antoninus Pius. Hadrian had the 51-year-old Antoninus adopt 16-year-old Marcus Annius Verus, who was to rule as Marcus Aurelius. Hadrian thus wisely chose not only his own capable successor but also the brilliant emperor who would follow Antoninus. In considering his demise, Hadrian had composed a verse of farewell to his own soul: "Little spirit, gentle and wandering, companion and guest, of the body, in what place will you now abide, pale, stark and bare, unable, as once you were, to play?" On July 10, 138, he died.

Extremely intelligent, bursting with energy and learning, Hadrian wanted to improve the governing of the empire and in the process of making changes alienated people. Dio Cassius, the biographer who, 80 years later, recorded the details of Hadrian's life in a compilation of imperial histories, did not always paint him in the kindest light. This may tell us more about Roman politics than about Hadrian, for Dio, a Roman senator and consul, held the usual senatorial bias against rule by emperors. Strong emperors, especially, he saw as usurping senatorial authority, even when, as in Hadrian's case, they treated the Senate properly. Dio published his history around 200, and it survived into the 11th century. The writer and scholar Pausanias, on the other hand, long after the time when flattery could have served any useful purpose, offered his own epitaph: "Among all the sovereigns, the Emperor Hadrian has done most for the happiness of each of his subjects."

HADRIAN'S LASTING VISION

The breathtakingly huge and magnificent estate that was established by Hadrian at Tivoli, east of Rome, although today largely in ruins, still reflects the emperor's astonishing wealth of knowledge about art and architecture. Already an energetic builder, he turned his retreat into one of the greatest creations of Roman genius. Developed over 15 years of Hadrian's reign, it spread across some 300 acres and was almost a tenth the size of Rome itself. The result, as a historian has aptly put it, was a dream in three dimensions—a vast collection of lodgings, baths, temples, theaters, pavilions, and other structures set among lovely gardens, ornamental reflecting pools, and refreshing fountains.

Hadrian, who had spent extended periods in Greece, the Near East, North Africa, and most of Roman Europe, was greatly influenced by his travels. Among other things, he developed a keen appreciation of Greek art and thought and filled the estate with Greek objects, including replicas of the famous sculpted caryatids from Athens' Temple of Erechtheum, seen standing beside the long, canal-like pool in the photograph above. But Hadrian was not out to mimic other cultures. The grounds and buildings are, in fact, the statement of an intelligent, well-educated man about the nature of Greco-Roman culture, expressed in the emperor's choice of art and architecture and in the layout of his buildings, gardens, and waterworks. All these were intended to convey by allusion the commonly held convictions and characteristics of that distinguished and invigorating heritage. Indeed, a guest joining Hadrian for a walk along the paths would doubtlessly have been invited to discuss history, myth, and religion. And yet while the estate was meant as a place of contemplation and inspiration, it also had its practical side, with accommodations for servants and guards, underground service passageways, and kitchens capable of feeding hundreds of guests at a time.

A VIEW OF PAST GLORIES

Even though Hadrian's great structures may now be no more than ruins, some remain recognizable and impressive, as in this aerial photograph, which focuses on the center of the rambling estate.

The circular building near the top of the picture is the Island Enclosure, conceived and executed as a personal retreat for Hadrian and the empress Sabina. Extending in front of it is the stadium garden, which once contained pools. To the left of the garden's upper end is the curved beginning of an enormous terrace, flanked by a high wall. Spreading beside the cypresses in the foreground are domed baths that Hadrian himself may have helped design; they daringly incorporate a variety of architectural shapes in a compact space. Partially visible at the bottom of the picture are still larger baths. And at upper right is a pool—filled once again with water— around which are the remnants of columned porticoes.

ELEGANT QUARTERS FOR GUESTS

When Hadrian was in residence, his estate became the center of the empire. This required that officials be present, along with the emperor's Praetorian Guards. Since the dignitaries could not coveniently travel back to Rome some 20 miles away, they probably stayed in the guest quarters. As the large photograph shows, only stubs of the brick walls of one such structure survive, but they indicate its design. Five equal-size bedrooms gave off either side of a wide central hallway, which led to a large common room. All had mosaic floors decorated with geometric, floral, or wreath motifs, as shown below. But while the rooms may have been comfortable, with niches for three beds each, they followed Roman standards of the day and had no running water or lavoratories.

HIDEAWAY FOR THE EMPEROR

The loveliest part of Hadrian's estate was—and remains—a small circular structure shielded by a wall and columns and further isolated by an encircling canal. Reached by bridges, the man-made island provided a refuge where the scholarly emperor, if he had been so inclined, could have escaped the hurly-burly of the complex at its busiest.

Called the Teatro Marittimo by the pioneering Italian archaeologists who began studying and excavating the complex in the 16th century, the mini-villa formed a complete unit of its own, divided into four groups of rooms, some with semicircular walls.

Around the outside of the canal stood a colonnade of marble columns that offered the emperor a constantly shifting play of light and shadow as the sun shone down on the marble and the sparkling water. From rooms devoted to bathing, he could climb steps and dive into the canal for a swim. And at the core of the building lay a small court and fountain, the quietest, most restful spot of all.

SUPERB FACILITIES FOR BATHING

With bathing an essential ritual of Roman life, the estate would not have been complete without its baths. The larger baths, seen here in two views, had tall columns and high ceilings, made possible by the use of vaults, that lent the facility dramatic scale in keeping with the elaborate bathing establishments of Roman cities.

These baths and the more intimate ones close-by had boilers to heat water for the saunalike sudatorium and its three pools. After working up a sweat there, bathers moved on to a tepidarium, a room with a warm pool, before taking a cold but bracing plunge or swim in the frigidarium.

WATER TO DELIGHT EYE AND SPIRIT

Hadrian's brilliant use of water in his landscape designs can be gauged in the 320-foot-long Canopus pool, at the far end of which *(left)* stands a half-domed banquet hall that holds the remains of a semicircular bench. The narrow pool may have served as a reminder of a famous canal that flowed between the Egyptian cities of Alexandria and Canopus. Once bordered by colonnades and statues—including figures of the Greek deities Hermes and Athena—the pool retains a few re-created figures (the originals are in a museum close by), notably the caryatids seen on the left in the view below.

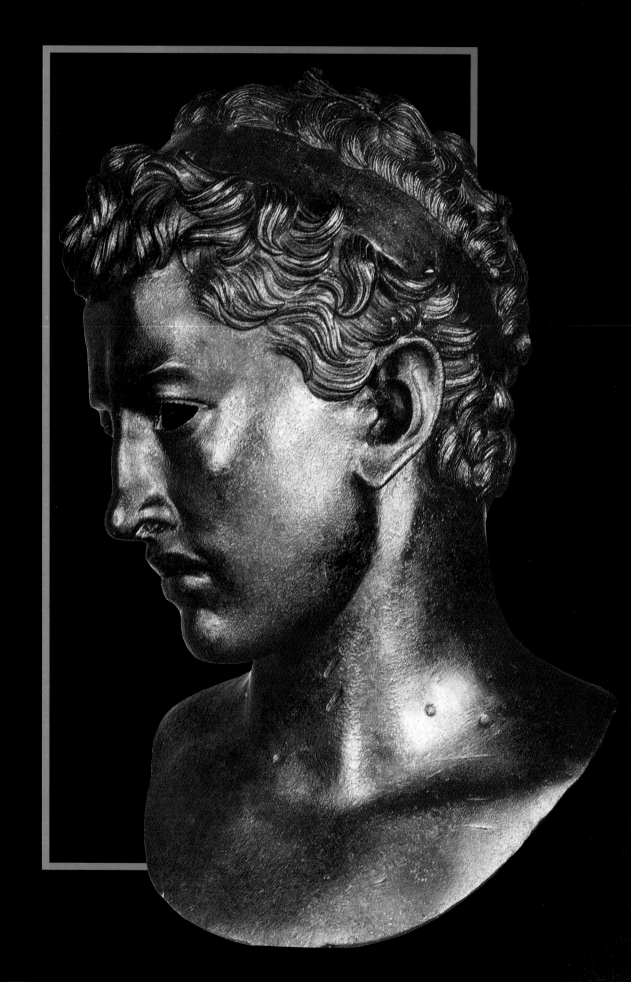

SUN-BLESSED DOMINIONS OF A TRIUMPHANT PEOPLE

Hadrian was one of the world's greatest travelers. Over periods totaling at least 10 years, he visited 38 of the 44 provinces that made up the Roman Empire of his day. He inspected the legions posted on the banks of the Danube and the Rhine and made the choppy crossing to Britain. Traveling far to the east and south, he gave audiences to his provincial governors and subject native kings in Asia Minor, Syria, Egypt, and North Africa. He brought more tangible benefits than the pomp and fuss of an imperial visit, for he put to work architects, engineers, artisans, scholars, and civil servants on hundreds of long-term projects intended to gain the goodwill and cooperation of the inhabitants.

These skilled workers built or repaired harbors and aqueducts, constructed public buildings such as theaters, libraries, and stadiums, improved towns by constructing new marketplaces and residential quarters, refurbished temples of local gods, and founded cities in locations that the emperor deemed ripe for development. Wherever Hadrian went, he left his mark in marble—and his name as well, in the Hadrianopolises that came to dot the map.

Inscriptions on the coins minted during these years of travel—which still turn up in the soil of Hadrian's domain—express his intentions. "The enricher of the world," says one; another labels him "the Restorer," while "Discipline" is stamped on a third. In AD

A colonial and a king, Juba II of Mauretania, today's Morocco, betrays in his appearance the Romanization of the peoples of the empire's North African provinces. Raised by the emperor Augustus, Juba wed the daughter of Cleopatra and Mark Antony.

123-124 and again in 128 when Hadrian visited Sardis, a major trade center, with strong ties to its Greek past, the mints issued coins commemorating his visits and styling him as the "New Dionysus."

But however strong may have been Hadrian's imperative to travel from one end of the Roman world to the other, the emperor would have been hard pressed to see, even in the course of a lifetime, more than a few of the many splendid Roman cities that spread from Asia Minor south to Egypt and west across North Africa to present-day Morocco. Today their ruins echo the glory that was once Rome's. Some have been largely erased by the centuries or lost beneath the edifices of the new towns that grew up on their foundations, but many—with such evocative names as Aphrodisias, Timgad, and Bulla Regia—survive as ghost cities haunted by their illustrious pasts.

It is no accident that the majority of these urban centers lay near the rim of the Mediterranean, which the Romans referred to as *mare nostrum,* "our sea." The Roman provinces of Asia Minor and North Africa tell a collective tale of prospering cities, knitted together by trade. Sharing Roman precepts of political and social life, they managed, nevertheless, to go on expressing their individuality in their customs and beliefs, which has much to say about Roman tolerance. Benefiting from their imperial connections, they at the same time gave Rome far more than they received. Indeed, in some ways, they made the magnificent city possible. The taxes they paid, the produce of their fields and orchards, the products of their industries, the output of their gold and silver mines and quarries—all these provided Rome with much of its wherewithal.

Like so many of the other cities of the empire, Sardis—whose ruins lie in western Turkey—knew fame before Rome rose to dominance. It began as a Bronze Age community sometime in the second millennium BC, growing rich from a local abundance of gold and silver. It derived strategic importance from its position astride the intersection of major trade routes of the ancient world. By the sixth century BC it was the capital of the kingdom of Lydia, where the revolutionary idea of minting gold and silver coinage is believed to have originated. The fabled King Croesus ruled there from 560 to 546 BC, amassing so much gold that he is remembered to this day in the saying "rich as Croesus." Later, Sardis emerged as the western capital of the Persian Empire. The Ionian Greeks set it to the torch

Three provincial coins minted in honor of visits by Hadrian suggest how far the emperor ranged in his journeys around the empire. The gold one above, marked Africa, displays a reclining woman wearing an elephant-skin headdress and stroking a lion. The silver coin at top bears the Latin word for Egypt and includes an ibis and a sistrum, a sacred musical instrument. The third coin, also of silver, is stamped "Asia" and shows a figure representing the continent holding a hook and a rudder.

in 499 BC, initiating two decades of warfare between the Persians and the Greeks. In the fourth century BC the Macedonian conqueror Alexander the Great seized the city, and Sardis would remain in the Hellenic orbit until the Romans took over in the second century BC. In keeping with its gilded legend, under the Romans Sardis established a reputation for textiles woven with gold thread.

Determined to find out just how much of the city's glorious past actually survived beneath the detritus of centuries, a group of American archaeologists under the joint sponsorship of Harvard and Cornell universities and the American School of Oriental Research arrived at the site in the summer of 1958. So productive did their digging prove that they would be kept busy for years, and their explorations would offer a detailed picture of what life was like in a Roman provincial city. Any modern visitor could see that a great urban center once thrived here. Mounds of debris cover about three square miles of the Turkish plain; from the extent of the city's ruins archaeologists have deduced that in its heyday Sardis sheltered more than 100,000 men, women, and children.

Some parts of the city had been explored in the 19th century. The German consul H. Spiegenthal, in 1853, probed the burial mound of Alyattes, father of Croesus; the British archaeologist George Dennis explored a number of tombs in the area between 1868 and 1882. But not until 1910 did a major systematic excavation, employing some 300 workers, commence under the direction of Howard Crosby Butler, professor of art and archaeology at Princeton. His imagination had been fired by two still-erect Ionic columns of the Temple of Artemis, and in five seasons, he and his crew freed the temple from the landslides that had largely covered it. He also examined some of the tombs honeycombing the cliffs above the city, but millennia of graverobbers had emptied most of them. A luckier man, Theodore Leslie Shear, an American who explored another Sardian burial site in 1922, made an extraordinary discovery: a clay pot poking through the crevice of a Roman tomb from the Lydian grave beneath. It contained 36 gold pieces from the time of Croesus.

Though the newly arrived archaeologists, led by Harvard's George M. A. Hanfmann and Cornell's A. Henry Detweiler, would have been delighted to discover gold themselves, they knew that the many occupation levels of Sardis would offer rewards enough. For one thing, they expected to find buried here remnants of the city that had been leveled by a cataclysmic earthquake in AD 17.

The Roman historian Tacitus had described how when the tremor struck "huge mountains settled, plains were uplifted, fires flashed out among the ruins." The stricken survivors immediately appealed to Rome, which, in establishing the empire, had taken on responsibilities for its maintenance and welfare. Rome would help other afflicted communities in the area as well, but "as the disaster fell heaviest on the Sardians," Tacitus wrote," it brought them the greatest measure of charity." Emperor Tiberius promised 10 million sesterces and the remission of taxes for five years. A high-ranking senatorial commissioner named Marcus Ateius arrived from Rome to inspect the extent of the damage and propose measures for recovery.

In time, a grander Sardis began to emerge. The calamity had created a blank slate for architects, enabling them to fashion Sardis according to their vision of what an imperial Roman city should be, especially one this important, poised between Europe and Asia at the confluence of trading routes that served the needs of both worlds.

In constructing new communities or renovating existing ones, Rome imposed an architectural scheme of its own, embodied in forums, theaters, baths, temples, shrines, plazas, markets, municipal offices, and law courts. Roman planners saw a city as a living

Built in Roman imperial style, Sardis' impressive bath-gymnasium complex, seen in an aerial photograph, places the city among the most opulent and prosperous of Rome's richest Asia Minor colonies. One entire side of the complex housed a row of restaurants and retail shops selling wine, paints, dyes, windowpanes, and glassware. The shops opened onto the city's wide, colonnaded promenade.

Reconstruction of the Sardis gymnasium's Marble Court was an enormous undertaking. Although 60 to 65 percent of the ceremonial hall's building material was recovered, most of it had been reduced to rubble over the centuries (right, above). The nine-year project required the use of dowels, lead, epoxy, and concrete to restore the remaining original elements to two-storied, colonnaded splendor (right).

entity, with public spaces where citizens could meet, conduct business, and attend to civic affairs. They connected these centers of activity with avenues and streets, some lined with colonnaded porticoes that provided shelter from the elements for the pedestrians and shade for the shops behind. Scattered throughout the cities were monumental arches, columns honoring Roman deities, and statues of men who had contributed to the glory of the cities.

The process of rebuilding Sardis, so generously funded by the imperial treasury, took more than a century to complete. Work on the Temple of Artemis, for example, began under Trajan and continued through Hadrian's reign and well into that of his successor.

Moving through the ruins of one era after another, the archaeologists examined the city's theater, its stadium, and various other structures, including a mosaic workshop. They dubbed their excavation at the city gate the "arch factory," for as team leader Hanfmann noted in a letter, "not a day goes by but a new arch comes to light." One site in particular caught their attention. It consisted of tumbled columns, niches, and arches. The archaeologists could not determine what kind of structure these had belonged to, and for lack of a firm identification, they labeled it Building B. Huge stone facades "toppled and twisted in wild mountains of marble" is how Hanfmann described the wreckage. Then one day, a pick worker shouted to the senior architect on the project, Tom Canfield. In the middle of an apse, atop a semicircular podium, the laborer had found the stone pedestal of a statue, now vanished. Canfield hastened over and brushed some of the dirt away. An inscription identified the missing sculpture as a portrayal of the man who had ruled Rome, jointly with Marcus Aurelius, from AD 161 to 169: "The Emperor Caesar Aurelius Antoninus Verus Augustus, honored by the city of the Sardians." The rest of the inscription told what the building was: "Claudius Antonius Lepidus, High Priest of Asia, First Treasurer, who from the beginning administered arrangements for the gymnasium, dedicated this statue." The imposing ruin, in other words, had been a Roman bath building, which by this time typically included a gymnasium. Here, the people of Sardis had done daily exercises, passed through a series of hot, tepid, and cold baths, and enjoyed leisurely conversation in a social atmosphere.

Baths existed in every town of the empire, and most cities had several. (Archaeologists have identified no fewer than 12 at Algeria's Timgad, whose population came to perhaps 15,000.) Some of these, built to accommodate hundreds (in Rome, thousands) of people, were enormous and richly appointed—palaces, for everyone to enjoy. In Libya's Leptis Magna, grand baths constructed during Hadrian's day spread over a seven-acre area. But there were also tiny street-corner baths and medium-size neighborhood establishments. In most of the large baths, including those excavated at Sardis, visitors could exercise in an open area called a palestra, working up a sweat by lifting weights, wrestling, jogging, or playing various ball games, before entering the bathing rooms.

Both men and women probably went to the baths, keeping to separate areas or attending at different times. Hadrian had ordered, in Rome at least, that the baths should be reserved for women during the morning hours when men were at work, and the rule may have applied elsewhere as well. A typical visit to the baths began early to midafternoon, at the conclusion of the business day. Relaxed social-izing was part of the experience. As they exercised or bathed, people chatted, gossiped, enjoyed the company of old friends, and made new acquaintances. There were rooms for massages, for the application of oil, or simply for strolling and conversation. Vendors often wandered about, supplying the bathers with food and drink. Most people stayed for two or three hours before heading home.

A vivid sense of what went on is conveyed in a letter from a provincially born government official of the second century AD named Lucian, who lived above a bath and complained of the noise: "When your strenuous gentleman is exercising himself by flourishing leaden weights; when he is working hard, or else pretends to be working hard, I can hear him grunt." On other occasions, "I notice some lazy fellow, content with a cheap rubdown, and hear the crack of the pummeling hand on his shoulder." The lodger also grumbled about the "arresting of an occasional roysterer or pickpocket, the racket of the man who always likes to hear his own voice in the bathroom, or the enthusiast who plunges into the swimming-tank with unconscionable noise and splashing," or "the hair-plucker with his penetrating shrill voice—for purposes of advertisement—continually giving it vent and never holding his tongue except when he is plucking the armpits and making his victim yell instead."

Not just content to investigate the bath-gymnasium in Sardis, the Harvard-Cornell group embarked on an ambitious project—the reconstruction of the entire complex—that would take them almost 15 years to complete. Observing his workers at the chore, Hanfmann wrote, "They were drilling and drilling, doweling, putting in reinforcing rods, building up slowly, bit by bit, the mighty shattered columns." But this was not as laborious as lifting the architrave pieces that were to rest on the columns. "They weigh," noted the archaeologist, "up to three tons and have to go 30 to 40 feet up in the air. Things get even harder when the lift is 50 or 60 feet." The great effort was worth it, however, for the results vividly document urban grandeur in the Roman provinces.

In the heyday of the empire, the complex sprawled over five and a half acres in the busy center of the city. Its architectural detail was as impressive as its scale. Multicolored marbles covered the walls of a two-story court from floor to pediment; some of the marble columns had spiral fluting, and others were topped by exuberantly carved capitals. The court had functioned initially as an area where Roman emperors were worshiped, but later it became an entry hall. Surrounding the exercise area nearby were colonnades paved with mosaics. Throughout the building stood sculpted representations of emperors, gods, satyrs, and much more.

Attached to the bath-gymnasium complex was the edifice that the excavators considered their most remarkable discovery—a synagogue built into rooms that faced the court. Originally, this had been a wing of the bathing facility, then a basilica, the Roman equivalent of a town hall. Sometime in the second century AD it became a place where members of the Jewish population in Sardis could gather to pray and read the Hebrew Bible (the Old Testament).

Measuring 278 by 65 feet, the synagogue occupied a highly visible and prestigious location and could hold hundreds of worshipers. Hanfmann wrote enthusiastically of "its gorgeous mosaics, its shining marble revetments, its high lectern flanked by statues of archaic lions of Cybele [the Lydian earth goddess], now reincarnated as symbols of the Lion of Judah." From what remained of the synagogue's original main hall, the archaeologists could tell that it had been paneled in marble and decorated with paintings and colored stone inlays in geometric, floral, and animal designs. Even pieces of a large marble menorah—a seven-branched candelabrum like that used in the Temple in Jerusalem—survived, complete with the name of the man who had given it to the temple, one Sokrates. It had stood atop one of two marble platforms, the second of which would have held the Torah (the first five books of the Hebrew Bible). Other menorahs turned up elsewhere in the building, incised in stone, cut from bronze sheets, and etched in pottery or glass.

Although many of the numerous inscriptions uncovered in the synagogue were in Greek (which remained the language of Sardis during the Roman period despite the fact that the official government language was Latin), some of them were in Hebrew. Most of them included donors' names, followed by the phrase, "citizen of Sardis." Eight of these were identified as members of the city council, usually hereditary positions accorded only to wealthier families in the Greco-Roman communities.

Jews had lived at Sardis since the destruction of Jerusalem by the Babylonians in 587 BC. The discovery of the synagogue was

The size and lavishness of the Antonine Baths at the North African city of Carthage, renamed Hadrianopolis during Emperor Hadrian's time, reflected the social importance of such facilities to the provinces. The 650-foot-long building boasted innovative architecture, imported marbles, mosaics, and a breezy site overlooking the gulf.

Public latrines, such as this multiseated marble facility attached to a bathhouse in the Tunisian city of Dougga, were a standard feature of most Roman baths. In some cases, stone channels directed a continuous flow of water under benches accommodating as many as 60 people.

important for the picture it provided of this ancient Jewish community in the Roman period—prosperous, prominent, and flourishing within the non-Jewish city. That hardly jibed with the modern view of the status of Jews in the empire after the Roman destruction of Jerusalem in AD 70. They had been depicted by scholars as an oppressed and downtrodden people, punished by Rome for their monotheism, fierce rebellion, and nationalistic aspirations, and increasingly displaced throughout the empire by Christians. The evidence of a thriving Jewish community presented by the synagogue, together with discoveries made at Jewish sites elsewhere in the Roman world, provided the impetus for a major historical revision still ongoing and much debated.

The discoveries at Sardis often may have been sublime, but they could be earthy, too. In the vicinity of the baths, Hanfmann wrote, "there appeared before our astonished eyes a magnificently constructed public latrine—with the most elaborate provisions for water and drainage, and a few marble seats still near their original position." The presence of many coins at the site caused him to speculate that admission may have been charged.

The grandeur of Sardis, so evident in its ruins, bespoke Rome's imperial ambitions, and Hadrian on his visits to the city must have liked what he saw. But how had the empire that brought him here come to be? "Remember, Roman, that it is for you to rule the

Its vaulted rooms decorated with paintings of hunters capturing wild beasts, the Hunting Baths of the Libyan city of Leptis Magna may have belonged to a guild responsible for supplying animals for Roman spectacles. Hunting Baths is an example of a moderate-size facility reserved for the use of private groups.

nations," wrote the poet Virgil in his first-century BC epic, the *Aeneid*, which dramatizes Rome's origins. It starts with the fall of Troy when the hero Aeneas saves his father and son from the burning city and sets out to found a new city. "This shall be your task: to impose the ways of peace, to spare the vanquished and to tame the proud by war." If that indeed was to be Rome's destiny, it took a long time to fulfill. In 500 BC Rome controlled a mere 350 square miles of territory. By 260 BC, after wars with various Italian tribes and with Greeks who had colonized southern parts of the Italian peninsula, the Romans had expanded their territory to about 10,000 square miles. Alliances soon extended their dominance over more than another 50,000 square miles. Some two centuries later the peninsula had been thoroughly Romanized.

But Italy was not big enough for Rome. Drawing on the manpower of their new holdings and rapidly adapting to the demands of naval combat, the Romans waged a series of wars against the Carthaginians—heirs of the great Phoenician sea-trading empire. Despite some serious setbacks, Rome took Sicily, then Corsica and Sardinia, next Spain, and finally—in 146 BC—Carthage's home territory along the northern coast of Africa.

Each enlargement of empire whetted the Romans' appetite for more, and each gain in tribute, taxes, slaves, and soldiery helped make continued expansion possible. Now Rome eyed the lands that had composed the three great kingdoms that had been formed from the empire of Alexander the Great shortly after his death—one centered in Macedonia, a second in Syria, and the third in Egypt. Between 146 BC and 30 BC, Rome seized them all. Smaller eastern kingdoms in Asia Minor and the Levant were similarly devoured. The islands of Cyprus and Crete fell under Roman sway, and, to the west and north, the tribes of Gaul, Germany, and Britain gave way before Roman legions. Under Hadrian, the empire, with its 44 provinces, encompassed some two million square miles of land. To maintain domination of such a vast realm required defenses along the Danube, the Rhine, the Euphrates, the edge of the African desert, and other frontiers; yet such was Rome's might that many of these boundaries would more or less hold for several generations to come.

Still, it was a complex world that the Romans had swallowed, with fractious and unlettered tribes to the west and the north, Punic and Berber cultures in the former Carthaginian possessions, and highly sophisticated urbanites in the Hellenized lands of the east that

A depiction of Berbers in chains dominates this section of a larger mosaic portraying the native peoples of North Africa in the heyday of the empire. Although Rome never fully vanquished the Berbers, a Berber, Septimius Severus, became emperor in AD 193. He had served Rome faithfully as a general in charge of Roman forces in the Adriatic province of Illyria.

90

Alexander had conquered. The Romans adapted to what they found with flexibility. They imposed firm control where necessary and governed with a light hand where force was not required. They put the west, with its combustible Celtic and Germanic tribes, under direct rule, watched over by a permanent military guard. But around much of the Mediterranean rim, the Roman military was barely visible after conquest or annexation. The seven African provinces were defended by a single legion of more than 5,000 men, plus auxiliary forces; Greece and Asia Minor were ungarrisoned.

The empire was essentially an agrarian one, with towns and cities serving as the focal points of power and progress—beacons in a vast sea of peasantry. Although the provincial cities were subject to governors appointed by Rome and, through them, to the emperor himself, local independence was considerable. In accordance with Rome's own ancient model of government, local magistrates and councils controlled civic affairs; because of their power, they eventually evolved into a hereditary elite. These officials were responsible for, among other things, administering justice, organizing taxation, and maintaining public buildings.

Even when the empire was at its height, most of the provincial cities remained small, with between 5,000 and 15,000 inhabitants. But a few centers had grown much larger. Antioch and Apamea in Syria may have each been home to about 200,000. Alexandria—one of 20 cities founded by Alexander the Great—rivaled Rome itself in size, with a population probably in excess of half a million.

Although Sardis preserved some of its Greek identity, by Hadrian's day it was a thoroughly Roman city not only in appearance but also in outlook, trustworthy and loyal. But there were some regions of the empire, including North Africa, where tribes resisted Romanization, especially since it meant for some giving up their nomadic way of life as herders so that their grazing land could be devoted to crops. In order to keep matters from getting out of hand, Rome built whole cities in some of its trouble spots for the benefit of retired legionaries, who might be expected to preserve their loyalty to the emperor while keeping an eye on the locals. Timgad and Volubilis, the latter Rome's most western settlement in today's Morocco, represent two such outposts. To make these cities as livable as possible, irrigation projects were undertaken, and aqueducts covering immense distances were built so the inhabitants might have fresh water.

A sprawling floor plan (foreground) attests to the wealth of the owner of this Roman house overlooking the sea in Tipasa, a city in present-day Algeria. The rooms were terraced because of the sloping site, and the lowest level, which opened onto the street, had several shops.

A later and perhaps more prosperous owner added several underground rooms to an already luxurious home in Tunisia's Bulla Regia. The renovation project also included the replacement of many of the ground-floor mosaics, updating the interior decor of the house according to the latest fashion.

Founded in Trajan's time in AD 100, Timgad was strategically placed near several key valleys of the Aurès mountain range. The Third Legion, stationed nearby at Lambaesis, helped control the unruly Berber tribes in the hills and lowlands. Though most of Timgad's colonists typically were not from Italy, they had become sufficiently Romanized during their 25 years in the army to create a city thoroughly Roman in its practices as well as its appearance. Its distinguished citizens, known by the statues erected to honor them, included Sertius, who rose to the class of equestrian in the army around AD 200. Upon retirement, he built a market, with shops for small businesses, and decorated Timgad with likenesses of himself and his wife. Vocontius was another distinguished citizen, similarly immortalized in stone, who had a reputation not only for having been an orator who spoke Greek and Latin eloquently but also for having displayed great military prowess during his army career.

In such towns, built from scratch, wealth gradually accumulated, and as time went on some citizens, such as Sertius, grew very rich; others, such as Vocontius, increased their stature by virtue of contributions to the city's culture. Gradually, a colonial upper class developed. The French scholar Yvon Thébert studied the growth and lifestyle of these people by examining the ruins of private homes in several Roman North African towns that had been excavated by French teams early in the 20th century. He discovered the inevitable—that as various individuals became rich and famous, they sought

grander homes. The tight rectangular grid of the traditional Roman city, however, hemmed them into small blocks of about 4,000 square feet, too diminutive a space for their aspirations. At Timgad, however, the wealthy found a way out of this dilemma; some of their homes well exceeded the size of one of these restrictive blocks. A portion of the city wall was torn down, and along a strip 70 feet wide that extended beyond the city limits, the enormous houses of the elite sprang up. This real-estate venture may have been of

Sertius' doing. Eventually many people, well-to-do and otherwise, came to live outside the walls of Timgad.

In other cities, such as Dougga and Bulla Regia in Tunisia, rich home owners simply gobbled up surrounding properties to create large lots. But a number of the wealthy residents of Bulla Regia took a different tack. They dug into the earth to escape the African heat, for the subterranean rooms were considerably cooler than those above ground. In doing so, they increased their homes' square footage with multistoried basements. But they may also have been following fashion, imitating the emperors on Rome's Palatine Hill, who in the first century AD built grand below-ground apartments.

As might be expected of well-to-do colonials, their houses showed evidence of frequent renovation and redecoration, with rooms and wings added or existing chambers' dimensions modified for different purposes. Old-fashioned mosaics were replaced by more modish ones, and stylish ornaments were constantly acquired.

Entering one of these homes through the columned doorway, a visitor came into a spacious vestibule intended to impress with its elaborate decorations. At the house's hub lay a courtyard, often surrounded by a magnificent colonnade. Adorned with sculpture and paintings or mosaics of birds, flowers, fruits, or marine motifs, the courtyard might hold a full garden or a just few potted plants. At least one fountain, pool, or basin usually brought the grace of water to the heat of the day. Inside the house, bedrooms, often interspersed with reception rooms, had raised daises for beds or spaces marked off on the floors indicating where they once stood.

In such wealthy households entertainment likely reflected the Roman custom, as described by the second-century AD author Apuleius in his *Metamorphoses*. Here a guest describes sumptuous tables spread with ivory ornaments and couches upholstered with gold fabrics. "Enormous" drinking

An intricate and realistic mosaic of baskets overflowing with flowers and fish covered the floor of a Carthage dining room, one of many examples of mosaic art custom designed to complement a specific setting or a patron's interest.

cups were of "flawless crystal" or else "gleaming silver or sparkling gold;" others of amber and semiprecious stones had been "miraculously hollowed out for drinking." The visitor goes on to observe the "skillfully presented copious dishes" and the serving of wine by "curly-haired young boys wearing fine tunics." The dishes at a banquet such as this would no doubt have included fish purchased at three times the price of meat and enjoyed in cities of the interior as well as those along the coast.

Women, excluded in much earlier years from such feasts, had gained the right to attend, a change of custom that spread rapidly throughout the Mediterranean area and beyond. According to Thébert, such private banquets served not only to show off the master's possessions but also to provide a setting for him to hold forth on various topics. With the consumption of large quantities of wine—probably of excellent quality—guests frequently engaged in behavior that propriety would have restrained in another social arena. Sometimes excesses occurred, but the usual trespass was of a verbal nature—intemperate language, outrageous remarks, or flowery flirtation with a fellow imbiber's spouse.

Hadrian's Rome relied on its provinces in numerous ways, most importantly in feeding the city's restive masses. Grain, olive oil, fruits, and wine flowed to the capital from around the Mediterranean, along with such other commodities as precious metals, marble, granite, fine woods, wool, furs, ostrich feathers, medicines, and much more—including exotic beasts that would be slaughtered for public amusement in the amphitheaters.

Though in fact only a fraction of the total production of the Mediterranean lands actually went to Rome, a good deal of the profits made overseas ended up there—and not just in the form of taxes. Wealthy provincials, irresistibly drawn to power and fashion, chose to spend their money in the capital. After Rome conquered the North African territories of the Carthaginians, rich Romans purchased or rented vast tracts of appropriated land from the government, farming it by slave labor for the most part, although there were also many small landholders.

One of the most bountiful of Rome's overseas possessions was Egypt, considered an eastern rather than an African province. Reliably productive because of the fertile silt deposited along the

A CARGO OF MISMATCHED BODY PARTS

In the summer of 1992, while scuba diving with friends off the coast of Brindisi, an Adriatic port in southern Italy, Major Luigi Robusto spied a foot half-buried in the sand of the seabed. Robusto, a member of the Italian *carabiniere,* feared the worst, but instead of a corpse he discovered a piece of bronze sculpture. Searching the vicinity, the divers spotted many more bronze body parts lying about.

Hired by the Technical Service for Underwater Archaeology of the Italian Ministry of Culture, archaeologists began the process of retrieving the pieces from the seabed. All in all, they came up with more than 1,000 fragments and two large, though damaged, bronze statues. (The crushed head of the larger one is pictured below.)

Analysis of the fragments by experts revealed some surprising information. The hands, feet, heads, and torsos were not parts of the same bodies and were, as a matter of fact, from widely differing time periods and origins. The artistic styles ranged from early Hellenistic to imperial Roman, dating from the fourth century BC to the third century AD.

Scholars conjectured about how and why the disparate sculptures wound up 400 yards off shore under 48 feet of water. The fragments were probably scrap being shipped to a foundry, where it likely would have been melted down, perhaps to provide metal for weapons. But what of the boat itself? To date, only a lead depth meter, a stone anchor, and some lead plating or hull sheathing have turned up, none of which can be identified conclusively as having belonged to the vessel.

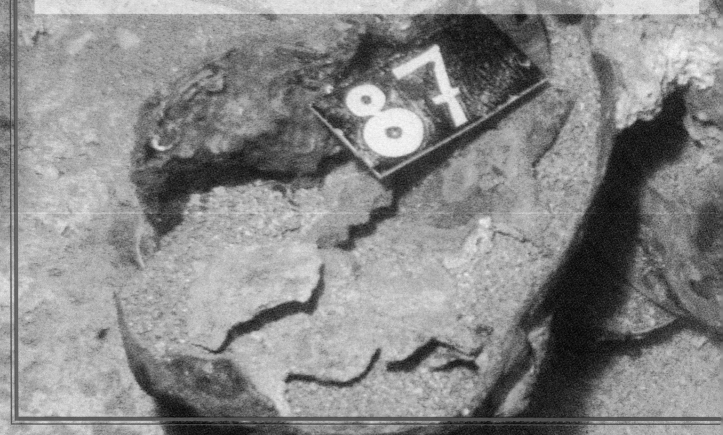

A long, graceful index finger apparently served as a support for a lance or staff held in this disembodied, larger-than-life right hand of probable Roman origin.

The head of a woman resembles busts identified as likenesses of Faustina Minore, spouse of Marcus Aurelius, emperor from AD 161 to 180. Noted for wifely virtue, she was deified. Engaged couples, hoping for a good marriage, made sacrifice before statues of the pair in Rome's Venus and Rome Temple.

This life-size bronze foot caught the eye of an Italian diver and led to the underwater discovery of the extraordinary cache of ancient bronze statuary.

banks of the Nile by the annual flooding, and with a large peasant population to plant and harvest the crops, it became one of Rome's chief breadbaskets. So important was Egyptian grain for the feeding of Rome that, from the time of Augustus onward, Egypt was administered through a viceroy and guarded by a full legion; two legions had been stationed there earlier. Hadrian saw fit to sail up the Nile in AD 130, and it was on this trip that his beloved Antinoüs drowned. But before the tragic event occurred, the emperor camped with his retinue near the famed Colossi of Memnon, twin seated figures, opposite ancient Thebes. He was drawn by the supposed miraculous singing of one of the statues, a phenomenon caused by the sun's warming of the fissured stone at dawn. In honor of the emperor's visit, not only did the statue emit a low-register, moaning sound before the sun had risen, it repeated the performance twice more after the early rays had arrived, which was interpreted as a sign of how much the gods loved Hadrian.

About to be dispatched by professional huntsmen, a leopard snarls his last in this detail of a mosaic from Tunisia's Sousse portraying a slaughter of wild animals in an amphitheater. An inscription accompanying the scene acclaims a citizen who put up the money for the public show and exhorts others to do the same.

Rome depended upon its colonies not just for wealth and sustenance but for beautification. The city's imperial establishment gobbled up stone and art from Asia Minor and Africa. A red granite quarried near the Egyptian city of Aswan, some 500 miles up the Nile River, and a gorgeous gray stone cut near the Red Sea followed the sea trail of Egyptian grain to the capital; both types were imported by Hadrian to Rome for the columns of the Pantheon's front porch. Egypt also supplied emperors with obelisks and wealthy Romans with sphinxes and ornamental statuary. Far more sculpture, however, came from the Hellenic lands, always viewed by the Romans as supreme in art—as the remains of Hadrian's Villa so richly attest.

One of the great exporters of marble and beautiful sculptures and carvings was Aphrodisias, in the Anatolian highlands of today's Turkey. The archaeologist Kenan T. Erim, a New York University classics professor, was drawn there by the magnificent ruins in 1961. Even a casual stroll through Geyre, a small winegrowing village that had grown up on the site of the city, revealed "in dusty alleys and courtyards," observed Erim, "beautifully carved sarcophagi being casually used as laundry tubs." The city had been named for the Greek goddess of love and fertility; as Erim gazed at the 14 columns of the Temple of Aphrodite still towering over the land, he found himself stirred by them—"the last wounded sentinels of a vanquished army" is how he described them.

Elegant Roman baths in Aphrodisias dedicated to Hadrian had been excavated in 1904 by the French engineer Paul Gaudin. But little further work had been done there until Erim's excavation. Erim used as a starting point an irrigation ditch dug by local villagers four years earlier; there they had exposed marble blocks and ancient sculptures. Before they could do any damage to the pieces or exploit their discoveries, they were ordered to stop digging by authorities, who realized the relics' value and significance.

One of Erim's early finds occurred after a rainstorm had washed away some of the soil in the ditch: "Suddenly I gasped at something I saw embedded in the side—and almost lost my balance," the archaeologist wrote. It was a marble head of a beautiful woman, wearing a headdress "with the shapes of towers and fortification walls." She turned out to be a Tyche, a deity who symbolized the destiny of the city, and Erim took it as a welcoming omen. And indeed it was, for Aphrodisias proved to be, as Erim could subsequently report, "so rich in archaeological treasure that choice sculptures roll out of the sides of ditches, tumble from old walls, and lie jam-packed amid colonnaded ruins."

From various historical records and physical evidence, such as signed statues, scholars already knew that Aphrodisias was the center of a major school of sculpture in the imperial era, and the scope of its activities now became clearer. Erim and his team unearthed a staggering profusion of marble statuary—some 200 wonderfully lifelike portraits of various worthies and of gods, satyrs, and mythological heroes. Occasionally the ancient inhabitants could be identified, thanks to inscriptions on the works. Among the pieces to which a name was affixed was a statue a former slave, C. Julius Zoilos, who served as a priest of Aphrodite and became a 10-term magistrate—and over the years grew rich enough to help pay for the town's theater. Sometimes the archaeologists found themselves unusually challenged, having to piece together a sculpture from broken bits of marble, using such clues as the stone's texture or chisel marks to help them match up fragments.

Romans yearned for the works made from high quality Aphrodisian marble, which came in both lustrous white and blue-gray varieties, and they provided ample business for the native sculptors, some of whom emigrated to the capital itself and set up shop. "Marble seemed almost malleable in their hands," wrote Erim.

Aphrodisias' marble carvers seem to have concentrated on the production of sarcophagi—and perhaps a few of the roughly 15,000 coins found buried around the city had been used to pay for them. These sarcophagi were marketed throughout the Roman world by traveling salesmen. Not surprisingly, the sculptors carved them on something like a mass-production basis. After chiseling fruits, flowers, and other ornaments into the surfaces and leaving room for inscriptions, the sculptors roughed out reliefs and figures intended to show the deceased and family members. By deliberately leaving the

EGYPT: THE JEWEL IN THE CROWN

In the year AD 130, the emperor Hadrian journeyed to Egypt. His first stop was the port of Alexandria, a city overshadowed perhaps only by Rome itself in its splendors. Then, much like a modern tourist, he took a cruise up the Nile to the ancient Egyptian capital of Thebes. (Julius Caesar had made the same trip, accompanied by Cleopatra, two centuries earlier.) Among the numerous wonders that dotted the Nile valley, the emperor's party seemed particularly impressed by the

two huge, granite statues known as the Colossi of Memnon (actually the pharaoh Amenhotep II), which, in Hadrian's day, were already 1,500 years old.

Hadrian's pilgrimage to Egypt reflected his—and his fellow Romans'—fascination for that timeless realm. In a political sense as well, the land of the pharaohs retained a unique position among Rome's overseas provinces: Since Augustus' reign, Egypt had been considered the emperor's personal possession. But beyond its fiscal value—the Nile valley provided the bulk of Rome's grain supply—Egypt also held a mystical attraction to Romans, whose particular brand of polytheism could always accommodate additions to its pantheon of gods. Venerable Egyptian deities—Serapis and Isis had large cult followings and temples dedicated to them in Rome—were especially revered, not only for their longevity but also for the opulence of the ceremonies attending their worship.

Roman respect for Egypt did not, however, prevent wholesale pilferage of sphinxes, statuary, and, above all, obelisks—one was set up as a sundial in Rome's Campus Martius—by a succession of emperors, though there is no record that the art lover Hadrian carted home a "souvenir" from his visit.

This exquisite second- or third-century AD Roman mosaic somewhat fancifully portrays the wonders of the Nile valley, from its headwaters in the Ethiopian highlands (top) *to the delta and Alexandria* (bottom panels).

faces blank, they allowed sculptors at the point of destination to finish the work with appropriate likenesses.

Excavations demonstrated that the busy citizens of Aphrodisias enjoyed their leisure as much as the Romans. Erim's team cleared one of the empire's largest stadiums, hairpinlike in shape and 760 feet long, with a 30,000 seating capacity; it had been used for footraces and other sporting events. Beneath the fertile soil of a lentil field, during the second season of digging, they uncovered a semicircular, marble-seated theater that could hold about 8,000 people on its stone benches. Comedies and tragedies were no doubt performed there—many of them Greek works, although plays based on events in Roman history or on life in drinking establishments became increasingly popular in the city's Roman period. Dramatists such as Plautus poured forth farces and pantomimes, often based on stock figures, such as a dimwitted politician or a hunchback gladiator, and dramatic offerings were sometimes interspersed with such crowd-pleasing stuff as boxing matches or the gyrations of ropedancers.

On an inside wall of Aphrodisias' theater, the archaeologists came upon inscribed messages from eight emperors—Augustus, Trajan, Hadrian, Commodus, Septimius Severus, Caracalla, Alexander Severus, and Gordian III. Augustus' reads: "I have selected this one city from all of Asia as my own," an honor secured by the municipality, indicating that it was imperially patronized. The emperor also ordered the nearby city of Ephesus to return a gold statue that it had taken from Aphrodisias. Hadrian's more mundane message is typical of the practical, hardworking emperor: He exempted the population from a tax on nails.

Just as Aphrodisias reveals how art and commerce were linked in the empire, so the city of Baalbek, a religious center located in present-day Lebanon, demonstrates the connection between political and religious authority. The Romans wisely solidified their rule in the various provinces by identifying their gods with local deities; often the provincials readily went along with this, associating their own gods with the more abstract Roman ones. Baalbek took its name from the ancient eastern god Baal, and its people were known for their spiritual ardor. The Greek rulers of the city had themselves related Baal to their sun god and changed the name of the city to Heliopolis, city of the sun. After the Romans took Baalbek in 64 BC, the eastern deities Baal, Adonis, Anat, and Aliyan underwent a sea

101

change and began to be associated, respectively, with the Roman gods Jupiter, Bacchus, Venus, and Mercury.

In accordance with their ambitions, the Romans built at Baalbek a colossal temple of Jupiter, their chief deity. Stretching 295 feet long and 158 feet wide and 130 feet high, it was intended, as one scholar has noted, "to outshine all previous sanctuaries." The architects set it on a platform constructed of what have been assessed as the largest stones ever hewn, lifted, or transported in the ancient world. The site they chose was already hallowed ground, for the mound beneath this base, recently excavated, shows at least three earlier sanctuaries probably dating back to the sixth century BC.

The temple gained added fame from the presence there of a so-called oracle, whose messages were expressed through movements of a statue of Jupiter when carried on a litter by local dignitaries. Over the years the oracle's reputation grew, even drawing Trajan to the temple in AD 115, on his way to fight the Parthians. Whether the oracle came up with a message for him is unclear, but after indicating that he wanted to know the war's outcome, Trajan was presented a broken centurion's staff wrapped in a shroud. The symbols could have been read as a portent of the emperor's own doom, for two years later, following a hard-fought, yet inconclusive war, Trajan succumbed to an illness and died.

Excavation of a theater in Aphrodisias, a city of ruins in today's Turkey, revealed its evolution over several centuries. Built in the first century BC for drama and dance, it was remodeled in the second century AD to accommodate gladiatorial contests. Still later, the theater's walls became part of the city's fortifications.

102

Shortly after a visit by Hadrian to Baalbek in 130, the citizens began erecting a second colossal temple, one devoted to Bacchus, the Roman counterpart of Adonis. It was excavated chiefly by the German archaeologist Otto Puchstein, beginning in 1900. Called by one scholar a "carved jewel," the temple displays, even in its ruined state, astounding mastery, with entire flights of steps cut from single blocks and stones fitted so tightly together that it has been said a razor cannot be inserted between them. Nearby, a small, round temple of Venus has also been cleared, and south of town, another temple dedicated to Mercury has been found, but of this only a monumental flight of stairs and a few fragments of columns survive.

While the old gods were thus honored, the Roman pantheon had to be continually expanded to make room for new gods—the deified emperors. From the days of Augustus on, most emperors acquired divine status by senatorial fiat, provided their successors approved. Their elevation would be followed by the erection throughout the empire of temples dedicated to their worship.

After Hadrian's posthumous deification, numerous temples were erected in his honor. In the 15th century AD, Cyriacus of Ancona, a learned traveler, came upon what was left of one such temple in Cyzicus, an island in the Sea of Marmara. Half of its 70-foot-tall columns were still standing when Cyriacus made a series of drawings of the building, raised on a platform measuring 100 by 200 feet and lavishly adorned with friezes and carved doorways. On the pediment sat a bust of Hadrian, the resident god. Its columns and podium remain today.

In the eyes of Hadrian, builder of the inclusive Pantheon, the empire could tolerate any number of beliefs, provided that they did not jeopardize Roman rule. But he was ever on the lookout for any threat to imperial cohesion. In his later years, he saw the religious zeal of the people of Judea as such a danger. In earlier days, Hadrian's views of Judaism had seemed quite positive, and he had shown some interest in the invisible god they worshiped without the aid of

The startling realism of Aphrodisian sculpture, embodied by this presumed representation of Hercules, brought much acclaim to the city's artists at home and abroad. Stylistic similarities have made it possible to identify the contribution of Aphrodisian sculptors to the beautification of other colonial cities, particularly Leptis Magna.

idols and with great intensity. Glimpses of the emperor even during his later travels show him amiably discussing the creation of the world with a rabbi and rewarding a Jewish peasant's gift of fruit with a basket of gold.

But Hadrian was well aware of Judea's religious scruples that forbade worship of the emperor and its resulting history of rebelliousness. The Romans had spent four years, from AD 66 to 70, putting down the Jews' most determined revolt—a war that embarrassed the Romans by its length, its ferocity, and the amount of resources it sapped from the empire. The war ended catastrophically for the people of Judea. Roman soldiers entered Jerusalem, set the Temple afire, and then rampaged through the city. "Pouring into the streets swords in hand," wrote the first-century Jewish historian Josephus, "they massacred indiscriminately all who fell in their way and burned the houses with all who had taken shelter in them. Running everyone through, they choked the streets with the dead and deluged the whole city with blood. So great was the flow of blood that in numerous instances it quenched the flames."

Though the Temple had been destroyed, Jewish hopes of its ultimate rebuilding had not, and Jewish rebelliousness continued sporadically in subsequent years. It may have been Hadrian's awareness of such defiance that prompted a set of anti-Jewish decisions. During his eastern travels in 130-131, he decided that another, more suitable temple should arise on the site of the Jewish temple—one that would make clear that Jerusalem was Roman and that its past was dead. The new temple would be consecrated to Jupiter. Jerusalem itself, still showing the ravages of the earlier war, would be rebuilt and settled by Greek colonists. It would be given a Roman name—Aelia Capitolina—incorporating Aelia, Hadrian's family name with the title accorded Jupiter, Capitolinus. The emperor's plans went beyond erasing the sacred city and the holy sanctuary; he also prohibited circumcision, the mark of the Jewish covenant with God. Defiance of the ban was to be punished by death.

Outraged by these assaults on their faith, militants of all factions throughout Judea united in revolt under a charismatic leader, Simon Bar Kokhba. For years they had prepared for war by developing networks of caves, storehouses, shelters, and hiding places. Says Hadrian's biographer Dio Cassius of the plotters, "They were quiet as long as Hadrian tarried in Egypt and again in Syria," but when Hadrian left the area in 132, "the Jews rebelled against him

Returning in triumph to Rome, soldiers display the sacred menorah and other booty from the sacking of the Temple of Jerusalem in AD 70 in a marble relief on one wall of the Arch of Titus. The Roman monument, which stands near Rome's Colosseum, commemorates Titus' quashing of the Jewish rebellion for his father, the emperor Vespasian.

openly." By subjecting the 10,000 legionaries stationed in Judea to guerrilla warfare, the rebels achieved some impressive initial successes. They took control of Jerusalem, threw up defensive walls to hold it against assault, and instituted, once again, their ancient temple ritual. They reestablished a Jewish government, minting coins bearing the slogan "For the freedom of Jerusalem." And they continued to harry Roman forces throughout the country.

Hadrian was determined to hammer the Jews into submission. He put a talented general, Sextus Julius Severus, in charge of the war, and legions were sent to Judea from many parts of the empire, even from vulnerable frontier areas in Germany and the Danube region. Severus answered the guerrilla tactics of the rebels with similar methods of his own, wearing the enemy down.

One scholar wrote that the Romans feared casualties, while the Jews feared defeat. If so, during the four-year war each side realized its worst fears: Severus laid siege to Jerusalem, captured the city, and razed it. One Roman historian estimated that 985 villages and 50 fortresses had been destroyed and a half a million people had been killed. Tens of thousands more had died of starvation or disease. Hyenas roamed through the countryside, feeding on corpses. By the tomb of the patriarch Abraham, in Hebron, Jews were sold into slavery. There were so many Jewish slaves on the market that the price for a slave fell to a fraction of that for a horse. And the Jews were further punished by a decree banishing them from their holy city.

The Romans suffered heavy losses during the lengthy war. Some scholars assert that the 22d Legion, transferred to Judea from Egypt, was annihilated, and at least one thinks that the Ninth, known as the Spanish Legion, was also destroyed. In light of the extremely heavy Roman casualties, Dio Cassius notes that Hadrian could not report his victory to the Senate in the words traditionally used: "I and the legions are in health."

In the aftermath of the catastrophe, the Jews, under the guidance of their rabbis, accentuated the pacifist strains of their faith and did not rise again to defy Rome. Three years after the war's end, Hadrian's successor revoked the ban on circumcision and other decrees unfavorable to the Jews but did not revive the Jewish homeland. Jerusalem was ultimately rebuilt, but in the form Hadrian desired—as a Roman city or, as one author has called it, "a forsaken, provincial town." Though Jewish communities thrived in Judea for centuries afterward, the Romans henceforth treated the country as if it had never had an ancient culture and religion.

Jerusalem today reflects Hadrian's plan—a typical Roman grid with its chief avenue still leading visitors through the city as they enter via the Damascus Gate. The Ecce Homo Arch, stretching across the Via Dolorosa, is the remnant of Hadrian's triple arch of triumph. Some scholars believe that besides obliterating the Jewish temple, Hadrian had a temple of Venus built over the Sepulchre of Christ. In 326 the Christian empress Helena had it torn down.

Aelia Capitolina stood for centuries as a reminder that the Pax Romana—the long period of order Rome brought to a fractious world—was a peace sustained by Roman might. Yet there were many subjects of Rome who felt no compelling religious impetus to revolution and who probably viewed the empire as did Aelius Aristides, a second-century AD orator and writer from Asia Minor. In a letter addressed to Rome, Aristides expressed his appreciation of the "profound peace" brought by Roman might: "All other competition between cities has ceased, but a single rivalry obsesses every one of them—to appear as beautiful and attractive as possible."

THE MANY OTHER ROMES

By the early years of the second century AD, travelers from Rome passing through Asia Minor, around the eastern shores of the Mediterranean, and then westward across the north coast of Africa toward the Pillars of Hercules would never have felt far from home. In every city along the way they would have encountered, as one Roman wrote, "a small image and copy of Rome."

The proliferation of Rome's image accelerated after Octavian's (Augustus') victory at the Battle of Actium in 31 BC, which ended the civil wars and led to 200 years of peace, the Pax Romana. Although many of the places Rome would alter had been under its sway for two centuries or more prior to Actium, the republic had been too riddled with internal strife to impose itself directly. Now Augustus Caesar, and his successors, could concentrate on the business of incorporating the far-flung Mediterranean provinces into a true empire.

Cities in North Africa wrested from Carthage during the Punic Wars and others in Greece, Asia Minor, and along the eastern Mediterranean that once belonged to Alexander the Great's empire found themselves united under the imperial eagle. A handful of towns, such as Timgad in modern Algeria, were newly built by military engineers on the Roman grid plan. Most cities, however, were revamped. Forums, colonnaded streets, basilicas, temples, amphitheaters, and luxurious baths were added to already extant cities. In Dougga, in modern Tunisia, for example, a rectilinear forum with its temple to Jupiter, Juno, and Minerva *(above)* was erected among the irregular streets, monuments, and temples of the city's ancient Libyan and Punic pasts.

Throughout the empire, Roman language and Roman legions were used to introduce and enforce Roman law. Roman currency bought raw materials and manufactured goods that would be transported on Roman roads or ships. And Roman architecture displayed a familiar and reassuring sense of order and control.

APHRODISIAS

Marble ruins of this first-century BC temple to Aphrodite still glow brightly. Noted for both its whiteness and blueness, the marble originated in local quarries that supplied the empire. From Julius Caesar—who claimed Venus-Aphrodite, for whom this city in today's Turkey was named, as an ancestor—to Hadrian, noble Roman protectors regularly expanded and glorified the city.

PALMYRA

Roman colonnades that once lined the irregular streets of Palmyra jut skyward out of the sands of Syria. Already important as an oasis and for its control of luxury caravans along vital trade links to India and the Persian Gulf, the "City of Palms" enjoyed spectacular growth and prosperity following Hadrian's state visit in AD 129-130.

LEPTIS MAGNA

The early romanization of Leptis Magna, a Carthaginian port in modern Libya, included this octagonal market pavilion built in 9-8 BC. The third-century AD emperor Septimius Severus, a native of the city, inspired massive improvements, including a new forum, a 12-mile-long underground aqueduct, an enclosed harbor, and the four-way Arch of Severus.

EL DJEM

This 45,000-seat amphitheater, the best preserved in Africa and among the largest in the Roman world, stands as a monument to the prosperity of Thysdrus (El Djem) under the Romans. Lying athwart major trade routes crisscrossing Tunisia and possessing extensive olive groves, the city excelled in the roles of importer, exporter, and middleman.

TIMGAD

Erected on a high podium, two of its pillars still standing, a temple stands surrounded by the ruins of the Roman outpost city of Timgad, in Algeria. Constructed by Trajan in AD 100 as a colony for veterans—to close nearby mountain passes to intruders—Timgad had all the amenities of Rome, including 14 baths. An inscription in the forum claims, "Hunting, bathing, gaming, laughing—that is living."

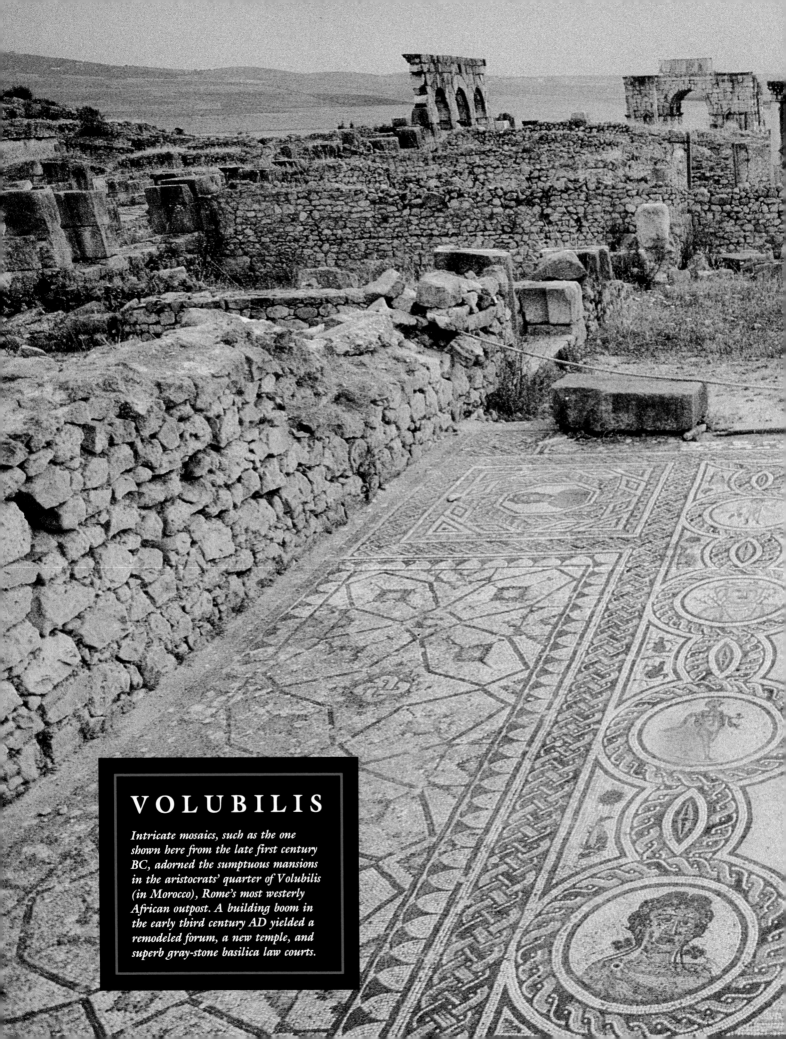

VOLUBILIS

Intricate mosaics, such as the one shown here from the late first century BC, adorned the sumptuous mansions in the aristocrats' quarter of Volubilis (in Morocco), Rome's most westerly African outpost. A building boom in the early third century AD yielded a remodeled forum, a new temple, and superb gray-stone basilica law courts.

THE ROMAN ARMY: A TOWN ON THE MOVE

Wearing a bronze helmet, a cuirass of overlapping bands of metal, a metal-plated leather kilt, and leg armor, a trim Roman legionary stands ready for action in this second-century AD bronze statuette.

The greatest monument to the ingenuity of the Roman army and its industrious soldiers climbs and dips over windswept moorlands, stretching across the neck of Britain like the body of a giant stone snake. This is Hadrian's Wall, named for the emperor who ordered its construction in AD 122. Built by Hadrian's troops, it reached some 73 miles from the Tyne estuary to the Irish Sea. Once it linked a chain of forts, watchtowers, and gateways that formed the northernmost frontier of the Roman world, a barrier to the fierce, unsubdued Celts and Picts of the north. This colossal structure was an unmistakable physical expression of Hadrian's policy of an empire with clearly defined limits.

The remains of the wall proper now rise no more than 11 feet above the ground. A V-shaped ditch, averaging about 27 feet in width and 10 feet in depth, ran along the base of the wall's north side. The wall itself, variable in its dimensions, typically was 6 to 10 feet thick, rising about 15 feet above the earth's surface, probably with parapets that extended some 6 feet above that. Thus, an enemy who was attacking at an inland location would be confronted by a formidable barricade that reached about 31 feet from the bottom of the ditch to the top of the parapet wall and stretched as far as the eye could see in both directions.

Throughout its length, at intervals of one Roman mile,

roughly 4,860 feet, stood fortlets now known as milecastles, which housed garrisons up to 32 strong and usually provided crossing points with double gates at their north and south sides. In addition, at every third of a mile, the wall included a large stone lookout turret, with perhaps a surrounding timber walkway.

Remarkably, three Roman legions, each with a nominal strength of some 5,000 men, completed the greater part of this fortification in only three years, most likely recruiting local labor for support work. No doubt Hadrian saw the wisdom in keeping troops busy; indeed, it had long been the custom to assign construction jobs to legions in a pacified area as an effective way of maintaining the efficiency and discipline of an inactive army.

More than a million cubic yards of stone were quarried locally

Extending from coast to coast near the present Scottish-English border, Hadrian's Wall here wends its way through the hilly countryside of England's Northumberland, an imposing reminder of Rome's once powerful presence in Britain.

and used in building the defensive line and its series of attached forts. Dressed and fitted stones concealed a core that was made of concrete and stone on the 43-mile-long eastern portion; the 30 miles of wall to the west were constructed of turf. Before Hadrian's Wall was completed, the builders changed their plans; along the barrier's south side they dug a huge earthwork that is now called the vallum. Here they made a trench about 10 feet deep and 20 feet wide, piling the excavated dirt and rock on either side in order to form continuous, roughly 20-foot-wide earthen ramparts. The vallum, following the line of the wall and broken only by causeways, protected Hadrian's Wall from behind, preventing the provincials from approaching it unobserved.

Initially, the Romans garrisoned most of their frontier force in already-established forts a few miles south of the wall. Later they replaced many of these strongholds with new forts built into the barrier itself or very close by. Eventually the wall included 16 such forts. Ruins indicate that each was laid out in a rectangle around a central headquarters building and contained a commandant's house, a hospital, slate-roofed barracks for perhaps 500 men or more, plus granaries, workshops, and stables.

Since even on this remote frontier Romans had to have their plumbing, there were centrally heated communal baths as well as latrines. The toilets consisted of wooden seats placed over a channel into which water could be poured to flush the waste into a refuse ditch. In the baths, furnaces heated bronze boilers that supplied steam and hot water. Besides cold or heated pools, the facilities frequently offered a saunalike dry-heat chamber and a steam bath and most often stood just beyond the fort's wall. They were the focal point of the soldiers' off-duty hours.

One of the second-century stone forts built south of Hadrian's Wall was known by the name of Vindolanda. Its ruins are located approximately two miles south of the wall's midpoint, and in the spring of 1973 the British archaeologist Robin Birley was leading a team digging at the site.

One day in a damp ditch, at the level of a timbered fort that had preceded the stone one, Birley was gently scraping between compacted layers of bracken and straw flooring when he uncovered two thin slivers of wood. Birley said they "looked rather like oily plane shavings," and he wondered if they indicated woodworking activity. On closer inspection the fragments proved to be two wafer-thin slices adhering to each other.

Carefully pried apart with a knife, the wood slices were found to contain part of a note that was written in Latin. "We stared at the tiny writing in utter disbelief," Birley recalled later. After some effort, the archaeologists were able to make out the surprising message; it referred to the delivery of "pairs of socks, two pairs of sandals, and two pairs of underpants."

Birley held in his hands the tattered remains of a letter written in ink by someone who had sent clothing to a soldier serving at Vindolanda around AD 102, six decades after the invasion of Britain by the emperor Claudius. The letter might seem little more than a touching curiosity, evidence that in Roman times as now, people sent parcels to loved ones serving in the army far from home. For Birley, however, it meant more. "If I have to spend the rest of my life working in dirty, wet trenches," he wrote later, "I doubt whether I shall ever again experience the shock and excitement I felt at my first glimpse of ink hieroglyphics on tiny scraps of wood."

Birley's enthusiasm was more warranted than he knew at the moment of discovery. His find led to the richest vein of documentation ever uncovered in the northern provinces of the Roman Empire. Over the next four years, he and his team uncovered more than 200 wooden tablets or groups of fragments that bore at least some writing. By 1988 they had assembled more than 1,000 tablets, including some 200 with readable Latin texts.

Several of the documents were so-called stylus tablets—thick slabs of wood with the center hollowed out and filled with a thin layer of wax to take writing incised with the point of a metal stylus. Most of the messages on these are illegible. Fortunately, however, the vast majority of tablets consisted of thin slices cut from the sapwood of very young birch or alder trees and inscribed in ink with a reed pen. When first cut, these tablets were so supple they could be scored and folded across the grain to make a closed letter, which could be addressed on the outside and then bound with cords. The largest tablets are about eight by three and a half inches, folding to about the size of today's audio cassette.

Opening the wooden tablets posed a serious risk. Upon exposure to air, the words on the first to be examined faded away. The writing, in carbon-based ink, could be recovered only through infrared photography. A better means of ensuring the ancient messages' survival was soon employed. The tablets were immersed in alternating baths of methyl alcohol and ether, which preserved the lettering as well as the wood.

This was the oldest group of written documents ever to be discovered in Britain, an unparalleled source of information about the Roman army on the northwest frontier. After nearly 1,900 years of silent obscurity, the Roman forces stationed in Britain suddenly spoke to posterity through this collection of writings—some of them official, some of them personal, some by senior officers, and others from the lower ranks.

Similar tablets had been recovered in smaller caches, but no previous finds had offered such a wealth of details concerning everyday matters. The Vindolanda tablets included, for example, a quartermaster's lists of provisions: local Celtic beer, vintage wine for officers, sour wine for enlisted men, fish sauce, pork lard, ham, and venison. There were also duty rosters assigning men a variety of daily tasks ranging from plastering to stints in the regimental bakery; personal letters of recommendation; an acknowledgment of a gift of 50 oysters; numerous requests for leave; a report detailing the where-

Volunteers and employees of Britain's National Trust—patiently observed by a dog—sift through the soil next to a section of Hadrian's Wall at Sycamore Gap. Here, in 1984, the diggers found Roman pottery, ironware, and stone gaming boards for playing Ludus Latruncalorum, or The Bandit's Game.

The third-century AD stone fort of Vindolanda (center) was the last of at least six garrisons that were built on top of one another in the early centuries of the first millennium. The original timber forts were each demolished, covered with turf, and then rebuilt, resulting in a succession of pristine layers of occupation for archaeologists to examine.

abouts of 752 men on a specific day; and—probably from the paymaster's records—a hoard of cash accounts and receipts for foodstuffs, clothing, and household utensils.

In one report, an officer complains about the nondelivery of goods, mainly cereals and hides. These apparently were scheduled to be transported by wagon, because he requested that in view of the bad state of the roads they should be sent by mule instead. Another writer noted bitterly how the "Brittunculi," meaning wretched Britons, refused to fight in the Roman cavalry fashion: "They are unprotected by armor. There are very many cavalry. The cavalry do not use swords nor do the Brittunculi take up fixed positions in order to throw their javelins."

Until the findings at Vindolanda, historians knew the names of only half a dozen people involved in the Roman occupation of Britain at the dawn of the second century. Now more than 140 names are known: the identities of numerous high-ranking officers and of ordinary soldiers, merchants, servants, and slaves, of specialists such as Vitalis, the keeper of the regimental baths, and Abionis the herdsman, and of the wives of several servicemen.

One personage of high station who figures large in the tablets is Flavius Cerialis, *praefectus,* or commander, of the Eighth Cohort of

Batavians, an auxiliary unit that originally would have been raised in the region of the present-day Netherlands. Some 100 documents bear his name or were written in his handwriting. Most of these consist of correspondence with his fellow prefects. On one occasion, Cerialis entreats a fellow commander named Brocchus to supply him with hunting nets. There is also a letter written to Cerialis' wife, Sulpicia Lepidina, by Claudia Severa, the wife of Brocchus. In her distinctively crabbed hand, Claudia sends greetings from her husband and her little son and invites Lepidina to attend a birthday party on September 10. The letter represents the earliest known example of handwriting in Latin by a woman.

Researchers have wondered why this trove of documents was left behind at Vindolanda, only to arrive at a very mundane conclusion: The letters were thrown out as trash. Evidence suggests that in AD 102 the Eighth Cohort of Batavians was transferred to the Danube and could not or would not haul with them all of the accumulated records and correspondence, although records generally traveled with the unit.

The soldiers also dumped in their rubbish heap large quantities of unwanted artifacts, primarily pottery and worn-out leather goods. Since some of the flimsy tablets show signs of burning around the edges, archaeologists surmise that many of the documents may have been blown from a bonfire by strong winds, landing on wet, cold ground, which helped preserve them.

But the historical interest in Vindolanda does not end with the departure of Cerialis and his troops. In 1992 continuing excavations at the site uncovered evidence of a massive oak-timbered

Found in one of Vindolanda's oldest levels, an ink-on-wood birthday invitation from one commanding officer's wife to another offers a rare glimpse of daily life on the British front. The woman's handwriting displays a remarkable similarity to demotic script on Egyptian papyri of the same period, indicating an empire-wide use of standardized penmanship.

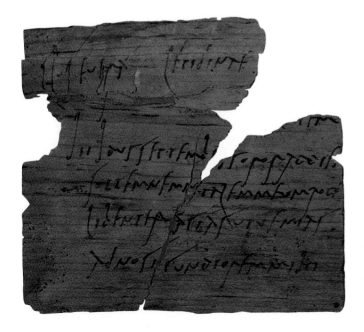

mansion, together with fragmented remains of wall paintings, woven floor mats, pottery, and implements. Experts dated the construction of this building to between AD 120 and 130 and judged that it may have been occupied by no less a dignitary than the emperor Hadrian himself, during his visit to Britain in 122.

When Hadrian arrived in Britain that year and ordered the construction of his great wall, the barrier's purpose was not simply to protect the Roman province of Britannia against attack but also to establish complete control of movement between Roman-occupied territory and the barbarian world outside the wall. Hadrian may also have been concerned that overexpansion might stretch Rome's military reserves too far. More significantly, however, he was pursuing his vision of the empire as a kind of Roman "fatherland." Within its borders provincials would have a sense of belonging to a social and economic framework that was in their best interests, and they would give their allegiance to Rome out of choice rather than fear. Hadrian drew the boundaries of the empire more clearly than had ever been done before, and the wall provides visible evidence of his determination to set realistic limits to the empire.

Rome's need to establish defensive frontiers in Britain and the Rhineland was no secret. The lessons from Roman military history were clear then—and still are. The Roman army was virtually invincible on open ground, with its close-ordered ranks of shoulder-to-shoulder infantry moving forward in successive waves. But fighting was always more difficult against guerrilla-style warriors such as those in the mountainous terrain of northern Spain and Wales, the hills of Scotland, and the dense forests of eastern Germany.

It was in the German forests in AD 9 that the western Roman army had suffered a shocking military disaster. That year the provincial governor, Publius Quinctilius Varus, led three legions east of the Rhine to suppress rebellious Germanic tribes, most notably the Cherusci. The legions never returned. On the long march southwest from the Weser to its winter base on the Rhine, the Roman host of about 20,000 soldiers—plus some 10,000 noncombatants, including slaves, women, children, armorers, medical personnel, and civilian tradesmen—was ambushed and completely annihilated in three days of bloody combat.

Before the late 1980s many historians and archaeologists tried unsuccessfully to find the exact location of the battle. Modern students of the bloody encounter proposed more than 700 possible sites. Then in 1987 a discovery by an amateur archaeologist led to convincing proof that the battle took place on the northern edge of the Teutoburg Forest, near modern Osnabrück *(pages 130-131)*.

The loss was almost insufferable to the Romans. Three highly trained Roman legions—nearly one ninth of the empire's legionary forces—were wiped out by relatively ill-equipped Germans. Many factors contributed to the debacle. Roman historians were especially critical of Varus, apparently a commander of limited military ability. He was foolish enough to lead his huge force, strung out in a column several miles long, through a narrow opening between a wooded hill on one side and marshes on the other, ideal for an ambush. A popular theory is that he was duped into taking the fatal route by double-dealing German collaborators. Certainly the Cherusci, led by their chief Herman, a former Roman army officer, appeared to be waiting for Varus. Herman and his men knew the territory; as one-time auxiliaries, they probably understood Roman tactics, and they may have had some Roman arms and equipment.

Faced with defeat, Varus and his senior officers fell upon their swords. Their remains were seized by the Cherusci as officers of lower rank were trying to cremate the bodies. They sent Varus' head to King Marbod of the Marcomanni nation in Bohemia, who sent it on to Rome. The shock to Roman pride was beyond measure. Indeed, the Roman historian Suetonius recorded that Augustus took the disaster so deeply to heart that "he always kept the anniversary as a day of deep mourning," and "he would often beat his head on a door, shouting: 'Quinctilius Varus, give me back my legions!' "

Shortly before his death in AD 14, Augustus instructed his stepson and heir, Tiberius, not to seek to expand the territory of the empire. His wish was observed by Tiberius but ignored by his successors. Yet the defeat at Teutoburg Forest had a lasting impact on the German front. Apart from punitive expeditions in 15 and 16, the Romans never again made a serious attempt to conquer the Germanic territories east of the Rhine and north of the Danube. Instead they erected the Rhine-Danube Line, a wooden palisade intended to keep out the Germans, which extended for nearly 200 miles, from the Rhine to the Danube. It would take another century of Rome's thrusting into new territory before consolidation, rather than conquest, would become the Romans' aim.

THE KILLING GROUND OF TEUTOBURG FOREST

As a British amateur antiquarian named Anthony Clunn explored a field near Germany's Teutoburg Forest one day in 1987, his metal detector suddenly emitted its telltale squeal. Beneath a few shovelfuls of earth, Clunn found the reason—a breathtaking cache of 162 Roman coins known as denarii. More searching revealed three lead balls of the type used in Roman army slings. Clunn did not realize it at the time, but he had found the key to solving an old historical mystery.

For when archaeologists led by Wolfgang Schlüter pursued the discovery, they were stunned by what they turned up in the surrounding woods and farmland: hundreds of Roman spearheads, pieces of armor, fragments of iron-studded shoe soles, bits of harness, many ceremonial and useful items, hundreds more silver and copper coins, commonly used to pay Roman troops, as well as a gold aureus, the coin shown in the background.

The coins, from Augustus' reign, bore his portrait. Some had images of his nephews Lucius and Gaius, or military governor Varus, on the reverse. All were minted before AD 9—the year an alliance of German tribes, led by a warrior named Herman, ambushed and slaughtered a Roman expedition of 20,000 soldiers and 10,000 civilians, commanded by Varus, somewhere in the Teutoburg Forest.

Modern historians had never been able to pinpoint the location of the battle. Now it seemed almost inescapable that this place called Kalkriese, on the northern edge of the forest, 10 miles north of modern Osnabrück, was the "treacherous terrain" described by ancient writers. Here, archaeologists concluded, was where three legions strung out in a vulnerable, four-mile-long column were trapped between swampy marshland on one side and a fierce enemy descending from a wooded slope on the other.

A few yards up Kalkriese Hill, archaeologists uncovered the remains of a rampart behind which the Germans may have hidden to surprise the Romans. There were no signs of combat uphill of the rampart, only below it, suggesting this encounter, among the most humiliating defeats ever suffered by Rome, was more massacre than battle.

The eight-inch-long iron point at left, above, may have been on a thrusting lance wielded in hand-to-hand combat by a legionary at Kalkriese. But the two at right were apparently on spears meant to be hurled from a distance, and their owners probably were overwhelmed before getting a chance to throw them.

This bronze buckle, two and a half inches long, was used to help secure a cuirass, the armor that protected a Roman soldier's upper body. The cuirass's heavy metal strips were bound together by leather thongs tied to such buckles.

The surgeon who possessed this instrument called an elevatorium may have died in the melee without ever using it. Made of silver-inlaid bronze, it was used to lift broken bones for resetting or for removing their splinters with tweezers or forceps.

Eternally enigmatic in expression, its vacant eyes a blind window onto the mystery of its purpose, this iron mask once plated with silver is held to be the most beautiful object discovered at Kalkriese. It is thought to have served a ceremonial purpose, perhaps as a parade mask for a cavalry officer.

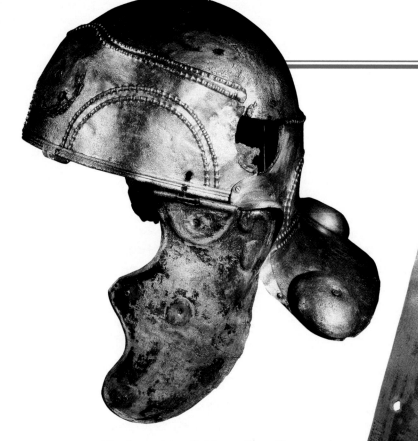

Yet in spite of this policy, Roman intentions sometimes seemed ambiguous. When Emperor Claudius led the invasion of Britain, he may have been trying to secure the empire's flank on the Continent against possible attacks from across the English Channel, as well as outmaneuver the threatening Danes. Thus it was that 4 of Rome's 27 legions crossed the Channel in an armada of probably 900 ships, carrying about 45,000 men, 14,500 horses and mules, and more than 450 carts for transporting supplies and artillery. Claudius himself followed shortly after, traveling in extraordinary style—with detachments of the Eighth Legion and of the Praetorian Guard, members of his family, an entourage of staff and courtiers, and a number of elephants.

Claudius personally led the attack on the capital of southeastern Britain, Camulodunum, the town now called Colchester. The awesome spectacle of legionaries in their flashing helmets and cuirasses of burnished steel, horse-drawn artillery, and not least, swaying elephants, never before seen in Britain, might have seemed enough in itself to bring swift surrender. It was not, however, for according to historian Dio Cassius, Claudius engaged the barbarians, defeated them in battle, and "thereupon he won over numerous tribes, in some cases by capitulation, in others by force, and was saluted as *imperator* [victorious general] several times."

Yet not all surrendered so easily. Several tribes continued to put up hard fights for decades afterward. Britain's greatest warrior-king, Caratacus, led guerrilla armies in the mountains and hills of Wales until AD 50, when he was captured and taken in chains to Rome. There he was eventually treated as an honored adversary and allowed to wander about the great city. Impressed with "the magnitude and the splendor of the houses," wrote the Byzantine historian Petrus Patricius, Caratacus exclaimed: "Why do you, who have so many and so fine possessions, covet our poor tents?"

It was a question that became increasingly pertinent, as the Roman army struggled for another 28 years to overcome guerrilla resistance in Wales. Moreover, in AD 60-61 rebels led by Queen Boudicca of the Iceni tribe inflicted enormous losses on the Roman army and plundered and burned three major cities in England: Verulamium (St. Albans), Londinium (London), and the old capital of Camulodunum, which had been handed over to army veterans to form the first Roman colony in Britain. And then the Romans spent decades in costly and fruitless campaigns to subdue the fierce tribes of Scotland. Between AD 80 and 105 alone, the army abandoned some 23 forts in lowland Scotland because they were repeatedly savaged by the Brittunculi. A more important reason may lie in the fact that Britain was one of the poorer provinces and unable to contribute to Rome's treasury.

Leather footwear worn by the Roman legionaries sometimes boasted iron-studded soles, providing durability and protection. This shoe and this sandal, found in London, possessed loops through which laces could be threaded and tied.

133

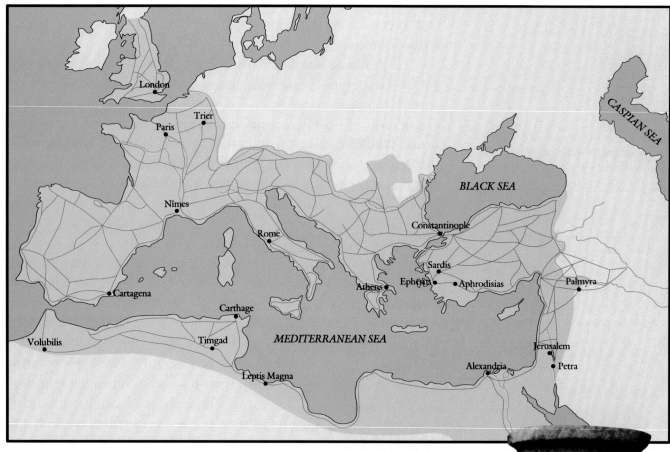

His long personal experience as a military commander and a provincial governor made Hadrian aware of how discipline and combat readiness could deteriorate in an army partly confined to a peace-keeping and, from his point of view, a "civilizing" role. The primary purpose of his tour of the empire was to radically overhaul Rome's legions. He wanted to tighten discipline, eliminate abuses, and encourage efficiency; all the while he endeavored to win the loyalty of his troops by his genuine interest in their welfare and his formidable reputation as a fair-minded commander in chief. He abjured the paraphernalia of his imperial status, refusing, for example, to wear a gold-and-gem-studded belt or carry an ivory-handled sword. And he was known to place heavy demands on himself, marching with the troops for 20 miles at a time while dressed in heavy armor.

The instrument that forged the Roman Empire—the army—was unlike any seen before: a fully professional, regularly paid military force with a capacity for both destruction and construction. Each legion was an efficient fighting machine of both heavily armed and light infantry, supplemented by cavalry. The troops used artillery such as ballistae, which hurled great stones 800 yards, and catapults, huge spring-powered, double-armed, crossbowlike weapons that could lay down a barrage of sharp iron bolts at a distance of more than 300 yards. A legion could move with remarkable swiftness to reach an enemy stronghold and reduce it to rubble. And the same legion could clear forests, drain swamps, dig canals, build fine roads, bridges, forts, aqueducts, dams, ports, and towns, and generally lay the groundwork for the expansion of Roman civilization.

For Hadrian, as he made the first of his great tours as emperor, evidence of this creativity was everywhere to be seen—in the towering aqueducts and solid bridges of Gaul, in the development of new towns, cities, and bath complexes in every province, and not least in the extraordinary network of well-maintained highways, which facilitated his comprehensive inspection of the empire. Altogether, roads built largely by the Roman army extended some 50,000 miles, from the Euphrates River in the east to the lowlands of Scotland in the north. The British lowlands, for example, formerly traversed only by rough trackways that were little more than footpaths, were now crisscrossed by new hard-surfaced, arrow-straight highways radiating primarily out of Londinium. That erstwhile hamlet was fast developing into the island's administrative capital. The routes leading north extended more than 300 miles, past the fortified Tyne-Solway Line—the future location of Hadrian's Wall.

The legionaries who had constructed all of these roads were Roman citizens—a requirement for service in a legion. A few of the more than 5,000 men in each legion formed a small cavalry contingent for reconnaissance. But in essence a legion was an infantry force organized into 10 cohorts, nine of them numbering in each about 500 men. The First Cohort was a special unit of almost double strength that included fighting troops as well as specialists and clerks of the headquarters staff. The ordinary cohort was subdivided into six centuries, or companies, each of which contained about 80 men under the command of a career officer, the centurion.

Still smaller units were formed by the division of each century into 10 sections of eight men—contubernia, "tent parties," so called because in the field they shared a leather tent. On the march, each contubernium was provided with a mule, which carried the tent plus construction equipment. According to the first-century AD Jewish

135

historian Josephus, this equipment included a saw, a pickax, a sickle, a chain, a rope, a spade, and a large basket for moving earth.

With these simple implements, the legionaries—sometimes supported by gangs of laborers—created efficient and elaborate road networks, which would remain unequaled for more than 1,500 years. Many of their roads provide the basis of highway systems used today in Britain. Thousands of miles of disused Roman roads can still be traced, some distinguished by surviving milestones—carved cylinders of stone up to a height of about six feet that record the name of the incumbent emperor and the distance to the nearest town.

Two famous Roman roads are still in use in Britain after nearly 2,000 years: One was renamed Watling Street, probably in the 11th century. Today it forms part of the Great North Road connecting London with Scotland. The original surface had long been covered by many layers of paving, of course, but part of the old roadway was revealed in 1973 when laborers, laying pipes near central London's Marble Arch, hit a two-foot-thick layer of flint and gravel. A second ancient road is the Fosse Way, which runs from Lincoln to Exeter. In Roman times it divided England into the settled areas to the south and the regions to the north and west where there was still military action against the belligerent Celts and Picts.

Apart from the engineering design and oversight involved,

SAVING A LONDON MOSAIC FROM LOSS

Roman London keeps cropping up under modern London. In 1976, during the renewal of downtown Milk Street, excavators came upon a beautiful second-century AD mosaic floor. Although some developers have incorporated Roman ruins into their new constructions, Museum of London conservators decided to remove the mosaic. They carefully freed it from its matrix, then reassembled and restored it for display.

After excavation by London's Department of Urban Archaeology, the 1,800-year-old mosaic is thoroughly cleaned.

Museum of London conservators painstakingly trace the mosaic's design to ensure proper reassembly of the pieces.

Conservators separate the mosaic into sections, noting the position of each loose piece before setting it aside for later use.

road building demanded unskilled labor. Roman legions were capable of more exacting work. Josephus aptly described a Roman legion on the march as a mobile town. And so it was—a force with the capacity to create and operate as a self-sufficient community. Every legion included a body of specialized soldiers known as immunes because their skills earned them immunity from routine duties. In the second century AD Tarrentus Paternus, a writer on military matters, listed among immunes: architects, surveyors, plumbers, medics, stonecutters, water engineers, roof-tile makers, glass fitters, shipwrights, ditchers, blacksmiths, coppersmiths, helmet makers, sword cutlers, wagon makers, butchers, and a variety of clerks.

With such skilled members, the legions achieved far more than conquest and the pacification of newly acquired provinces. They brought an economically sophisticated way of life to previously undeveloped parts of the world—building aqueducts to nurture the growth of towns and cities with water carried over long distances, introducing new products and manufacturing skills, boosting the development of trade and commerce by way of their great roadworks, and generally encouraging urbanization and settlement.

From the moment they entered new territory, legionaries followed a rigidly disciplined routine. First, at the end of a day's march, they established a securely defended position. In the words of

A piece of canvas is laid over each of the sections, and more adhesive is applied to secure it to the surface of the mosaic.

When the adhesive is completely dry, a conservator peels the canvas and the attached section away from the mosaic's base.

Museum workers transfer the mosaic segment, still bonded firmly to its canvas support, to a wooden pallet for transport.

At the Museum of London, a conservator reassembles the sections of the Milk Street mosaic, readying it for exhibition.

Flavius Vegetius Renatus, author of a fourth-century AD military manual, "When the Roman army camps for the night, it builds a defended city." Only a few traces of these march camps are still visible to the naked eye at ground level, but in recent decades aerial surveys of Britain have revealed previously unsuspected sites. Infrared photography, which accentuates tonal variation in vegetation, displays the precise pattern of defensive ditches dug almost 2,000 years ago. Through this means the location of one such camp, probably used during a campaign in Wales, has been spotted in the open countryside along the Welsh border.

Although they varied in size, march camps set the basic pattern for the permanent forts that the Romans constructed later. The soldiers built their forts to a rectangular plan similar to that of their temporary camps, with entrances about midway along each side and guard points at intervals along the ramparts and at the corners. For this permanent construction, however, the soldiers applied all their skills, creating stone and timber fortress walls and towers, fitting buildings with snug, long-wearing slate roofs, installing elaborate plumbing systems, heated baths, and glass windows. Remains at various sites indicate that the commander's house commonly incorporated its own bath and hypocaust, a heating system in which hot air from a furnace was circulated between two floors, the upper raised one to three feet above the lower; sometimes heat from the floor would rise through tile flues in the walls.

It was at this stage, following the establishment of a permanent military presence, that the Roman army began to work its enormous influence on local civilian life. Wherever troops settled, they immediately attracted opportunists seeking to profit by catering to their needs. Near every new fort there sprang up, almost overnight, a small civilian settlement known as a *vicus,* the term for a street of houses, which could also be used to refer to settlements of various sizes. Initially, the vicus would be no more than a shanty village, comprising some wooden shacks, a few shops, an inn, and perhaps a brothel. But where forts were occupied for many decades, even centuries, the vicus grew into a town with a substantial population and many permanent buildings.

In the vicus, soldiers, forbidden to marry legally, frequently set up common-law arrangements, developed lasting relationships, and established families. As a result, they chose to settle nearby when they were discharged after 25 years' service. They then took their

Military deities Mars and Hercules flank an inscribed tablet crediting Rome's 20th Legion for the building of a fort at High Rochester, north of Hadrian's Wall. The legion's symbol, a boar, lies at the base of the inscription. Similar memorials along the wall celebrate not only gods but wives and officials as well.

skills into the local civilian world and passed those skills on to their sons, who in turn joined the army.

The development of a vicus into a town was a long, haphazard process. The dramatic spur to urbanization came when the Romans began to establish citizen colonies in the provinces by settling large groups of veteran legionaries and civilians in designated locations. Such colonies had begun to appear late in the second century BC, in Gaul and the intensely militarized Rhineland and later in Britain not only at Colchester but also at Lincoln and Gloucester.

In addition, Rome began to recognize some other, long-existing towns as colonies, as a reward for their loyalty or for achieving a high degree of Romanization in their appearance, economy, and way of life. It was a coveted distinction to be able to include in the town's title such words as *municipium* and *colonia,* and towns worked hard to earn recognition. These settlements often counted among their residents many retired legionaries. Sometimes a provincial governor, who also commanded the Roman army in the province, directly subsidized the development of a colonial city by assigning military architects, artisans, and soldiers to its construction.

From the writings of Tacitus and other historians, it is known that over the years the numbers of Roman legions varied, ranging from 25 early in the first century to a maximum of 33 two centuries later. It is sometimes possible to establish precisely where legions were stationed at any given time because they left behind stone inscriptions on their constructions. These generally record the military unit involved and the name of the incumbent emperor and provincial governor. Some commemorate events of importance to the legion such as the arrival of reinforcements. At Hadrian's Wall, for example, hundreds of inscriptions on milecastles, forts, and the wall itself record the work carried out by the second, sixth, and 20th legions. Cohorts and centuries left their hallmarks on the wall sections they built. Moreover, as shown by a find at the legionary fortress of Chester, the army even left such commemorative pronouncements on the lead piping it installed.

These inscriptions indicated to a future inspector which army elements were responsible for a specific achievement and were therefore a method of quality control. Carved on stone or wooden plaques, sometimes only fragments of the inscriptions remain, which are hard to interpret. Others have been lost or moved; reused stones have occasionally cropped up, having been used in the construction of farmhouses.

While invaluable for tracking the movement and activities of Roman legions, such carvings also provide information about the other soldiers who helped expand the Roman Empire and defend its frontiers, the *auxilia,* or auxiliaries. These units were manned by troops who were not Roman citizens but drawn from many different provinces. They were trained by the legions but remained in units of their own, bolstering border defense as they served on the frontier with the legions. By the latter half of the first century AD, auxiliaries included Spaniards, Hungarians, Germans, Gauls, Britons, Greeks, Syrians, and Egyptians.

Knowledge of the achievements of the auxilia is limited because Roman historians preferred to describe the legions' work. Also, the auxiliaries were not subject to detailed recordkeeping to the same extent as the legions. But Dio Cassius tells that on at least one major campaign—the invasion of Britain in AD 43 —the legions were equaled in numerical strength by auxiliary units. And a commemoration of their efforts can be found on stone plaques on forts along the Antonine Wall, a 36-mile-long turf barrier built about 100 miles north of Hadrian's Wall and completed around 145. Writings there indicate that auxiliaries engaged in fort-building efforts. Auxiliaries were organized in cohorts ranging in strength from 500 to 1,000 men and were of three

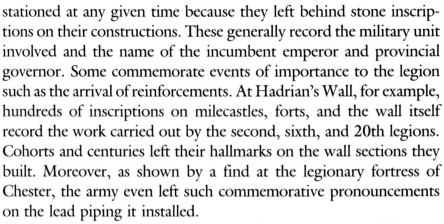

The narrative of Trajan's Column, while commemorating the emperor's victory over Dacia (modern Romania), provides a glimpse into army life. The section seen here depicts an auxiliary cavalryman riding into battle as others stand, brandishing Dacian heads.

This scene portrays legionary and auxiliary soldiers fighting side by side against the Dacians. Legionaries and auxiliaries endured a form of boot camp during their training, complete with drill instructors, stone-slinging lessons, and, since there were no stirrups, instruction in mounting horses.

basic types—*peditatae* (infantry), *alae* (cavalry), and units combining both elements.

Roman commanders carefully preserved the national identities of some auxiliary units in order to maintain their specialist skills, useful in combat. The Sarmatians of what is now Poland and the Thracians of the Balkan Peninsula were expert mounted spearmen, and Syrians took lethal aim with their deadly composite bows made of glued-together layers of horn, wood, and sinew. Syrian archers were so highly valued that their sons by local women were not allowed to join their unit, despite any skill they may have picked up from their fathers; instead, the Romans enlisted more bowmen from Syria.

Scholars have long believed that auxiliary foot soldiers received in pay only about five-sixths what their legionary counterparts got, based on the writings of ancient Roman historians. Auxiliary cavalrymen, however, serving in a unit combining riders and foot soldiers, were paid the same wages as legionary foot soldiers. This parity was deduced from a pay receipt, part of a cache of more than 600 stylus writing tablets—similar to the wax-coated ones found at Vindolanda—which were unearthed in the early part of the 20th century at Vindonissa, a Roman fortress in Switzerland. The receipt had been written by a rider named Clua, stationed at Vindonissa in AD 38, who received 900 sesterces a year, an amount equal to what historians Tacitus and Suetonius indicated was earned by a legionary. Hadrian's troops were paid more than the rider Clua, however, for according to the historians, in AD 84 the emperor Domitian raised the army's annual pay by a third to 1,200 sesterces, the equivalent of more than 10 pounds of silver.

Auxiliaries were not conscripts but volunteers who enlisted, usually in their teens, for 25 years of service. They joined for the security and regular pay and, above all, for the reward of Roman citizenship on completion of their service, plus perhaps a modest pension and a small grant of land. Citizenship had many privileges.

As a veteran, the retired auxiliary was immune from taxation and had the right of *conubium*. This right enabled him to marry a noncitizen and still pass on his citizenship to his children, with the opportunities conferred by this status for advancement in the service of the state.

The auxiliary as well as the legionary received a military diploma upon retirement, recorded on two small leaves of inscribed bronze. Over the years, hundreds of these artifacts have been discovered throughout the empire, providing invaluable information about the disposition of forces at different times. For example, one military diploma, found at a fort at Chesters on Hadrian's Wall, records the grant of citizenship to men from 14 named auxiliary units stationed in Britain in 146.

After Hadrian built his wall, occupied Britain settled down as a loyal and relatively peaceful province of Rome, even though conflict continued on the fringes of the empire. During most of the period of Roman rule, as Sir Winston Churchill would observe centuries later,

A sketch of the interior of London's basilica, based on archaeological excavation, conveys the grandeur and monumentality of the largest great hall (500 feet long) of any Roman city north of Italy. The basilica served as town hall and courthouse.

Britain "enjoyed in many respects the happiest, most comfortable and most enlightened times its inhabitants have had." Another British scholar was more specific about what the Romans had to offer: Upon unearthing one of the many radiant-heated Roman baths found in England, he remarked that no one in that country had been as comfortable in wintertime since Roman days.

For the first time, all of lowland Britain—now united under one government and by approximately 2,500 miles of Roman roads—was free of constant intertribal warfare. The standard of living advanced dramatically as trade and industry boomed. The three cities burned in the rebellion of the Iceni queen Boudicca were rebuilt on a grander scale. Numerous towns boasted sewers, piped-water supplies, public baths, architecturally impressive administrative buildings, amphitheaters for civic ceremonies and games, spacious marketplaces, and stone shopping arcades.

The Romans usually appointed a town council composed of the wealthiest tribal members, who, on taking various public offices, were granted Roman citizenship. These local native nobles soon grew accustomed to the comfort and elegance of Roman-style living. Eventually the descendants of rebel chieftains were occupying luxurious villas with dining rooms, wall paintings, mosaics, imported furnishings, and heated baths; and they in turn set an example for lesser folk by adopting Roman dress and learning to speak Latin.

Tacitus, a champion of older virtues, wrote acidly about such changes. "In place of distaste for the Latin language came a passion to command it. In the same way our national dress came into favor and the toga was everywhere to be seen. And so the Britons were gradually led on to the amenities that make vice agreeable—arcades, baths and sumptuous banquets. They spoke of such novelties as 'civilization', when really they were only a feature of enslavement."

But for those who saw Romanization in a less cynical light, there was the tangible benefit of citizenship. The great merit of Roman colonization was that it was remarkably nondiscriminatory. In Britain, as throughout the empire, conquered peoples were so fully integrated within the Roman system that there was no limit to how far they or their descendants might advance themselves after gaining citizenship. Men of non-Roman origin—Spaniards, Gauls, Africans, and Germans—rose to become consuls, provincial governors, and even emperors.

Among those who prospered mightily during Britain's long

Pax Romana was the family of the Faustini. Wealthy and powerful, these aristocratic landowners lived for at least 200 years at Villa Faustini—the name of both their country residence, near what is now the Norfolk-Suffolk border, and the village that grew up close by, present-day Scole in Norfolk. From treasures and artifacts the Faustini left behind, there is speculation that they were of the senatorial class, with imperial connections, and that family members may have served in far-flung parts of the empire, including Byzantium. They apparently converted to Christianity sometime in the fourth century.

The Faustini were probably an example of provincials who made good accepting Romanization. During much of their third- and fourth-century heyday, they and other prosperous Romano-Britons fared well on their remote island, perhaps better than they would have done in Rome. For in these times the imperial government was steeped in corruption and beset by military near anarchy. In the years between 235 and 284, Rome had 21 emperors, only two of whom died of natural causes. Emperors repeatedly debased the currency to pay for wars or enrich themselves, causing inflation that pushed the empire to the brink of bankruptcy. Legions battled against legions in internecine warfare, and amid the turmoil barbarian tribes were able to pour across undefended frontiers on the Rhine and the Danube, while Persia attacked from the east, so creating wars on two fronts. Yet throughout this time of intermittent anarchy, many services functioned normally in Rome as elsewhere.

Late in the third century, an emperor named Diocletian managed to stem the imperial bleeding, and his reforms held, although they could not prevent the coming tidal wave of invasions. But his reign also saw the beginnings of the breakup of the Roman Empire. In 286 Diocletian promoted one of his officers, Maximian, as co-emperor to rule the empire's western part; later two younger officers, Galerius and Constantius, were appointed to succeed Diocletian and Maximian, respectively, as rulers over east and west.

Constantius' son Constantine rose to power in the west upon the death of his father, and several years later, in 324, established himself as sole emperor, defeating all other contenders. Before then, however, Constantine took the momentous step of converting to Christianity and in 313 proclaimed toleration of Christianity as a growing religion. On the site of the ancient city of Byzantium, he established Constantinople, which he called the "new Rome," free of pagan cults and worthy to be the center of the empire. From this time

The spring that fed the luxurious pools and basins of Bath, England, still produces thousands of gallons a day of 122 degrees F. mineral water. Called Aquae Sulis, or Waters of Sul, after a Celtic god, the Roman spa drew bathers for more than 300 years for its supposed curative powers. Visitors seeking a little extra medical help often tossed offerings of coins and jewelry into the water.

on there would be not merely two parts to the empire, and frequently two emperors, but two capitals as well. The decline of the Western Roman Empire would proceed at a varying rate over the next two centuries until, finally, Rome fell to the Goths in 470; the eastern center, based in Constantinople, however, survived in the Byzantine Empire until 1453.

The question of why Rome itself fell, and with it the Western Empire, has been debated through the centuries. More than 200 factors have been cited as contributory causes. They have ranged from the predictable—including political intrigue, economic mismanagement, religious division, corruption, top-heavy bureaucracy, immorality, and civil wars—to the surprising, such as climatic change and the recently discredited theory of widespread mental erosion caused by poisoning from lead water pipes and eating utensils.

But Rome's most damaging problems may all have sprung from the same root causes: overexpansion of the empire—which led to too great a dependence on conquered peoples for economic and military support—coupled with poor fiscal management. Later campaigns beyond the frontiers set by Hadrian put great stress on Rome's economic resources and exposed the empire to barbarian attack. By the beginning of the fourth century there was no longer any marked distinction between citizen legionaries and auxiliaries. Moreover, non-Romans, mainly Germans, now provided most of the empire's defense. By late in the fourth century barbarians, wildly ferocious Visigoths among them, were recruited *en bloc* to fight alongside the Roman army. Often they were untrained and served under their own commanders. Discipline and effective training had made the Roman army the most efficient fighting force the world had ever seen. Now these key strengths were diluted as legionaries became infected by the lax attitudes of their barbarian allies.

There were plenty of enemies to fight. Throughout the fourth century wave upon wave of barbarian tribes crashed against the northern frontiers of Gaul and Italy, mounting into a tidal wave that finally engulfed the entire Western Empire. From Central Asia came the Alans and the Huns, and from north of the Rhine and the Danube a wide range of Germanic peoples—Visigoths, Vandals, Franks, Burgundians, Suebi, and Alamanni.

On the last day of 406 a vast horde of Teutons, Suebi, Alans, Vandals, and Burgundians crossed the frozen Rhine and swept southwest through Gaul, leaving every major city in flames. They

Retired Suffolk gardener Eric Lawes poses with the metal detector he was using when he stumbled upon a massive hoard of Roman treasure. Although the cache contained jewelry and tableware, it consisted primarily of coins—nearly 15,000 of them. Below, British Museum curator Catherine Johns holds some of the coins, which have been identified as the products of 16 different mints, suggesting that currency flowed freely throughout the Roman Empire.

were apparently unopposed. Rome's Rhineland army had long since been withdrawn to help defend Italy against the Visigoths, invaders so menacing that Emperor Honorius had moved his court to the supremely well-protected port of Ravenna on the Adriatic. The forts at Hadrian's Wall show signs of having been abandoned by the military some time around 400; perhaps it happened in 407, when a usurper arose in Britain and took the title of Emperor Constantine. He seized command of all Roman troops in Britain and led them across the Channel, where he managed to regain western and northern Gaul from Germanic tribes—but for his own purposes, rather than as a service to the emperor Honorius.

The departure of the troops left Britannia undefended, and the economy, which depended on the army, undermined. Picts, along with Celts from Ireland, were soon raiding the northern regions, and the very next year a massive invasion by Saxons from the Continent threatened the continued existence of Roman civilization in Britain. The Faustini may well have been among the provincial leaders who organized a citizens' militia to hold the invaders at bay as long as possible. It was a losing battle and became particularly discouraging in 410 when Honorius sent a letter urging the defenders to fight on but declaring there was no way he could help. Soon thereafter Rome fell to the Visigoths, who, after three days of looting and wanton savagery, moved on to seek new conquests.

At around this time, the Faustini probably decided to take extraordinary measures to protect at least some of their wealth. Perhaps with the aid of trusted servants, they did what fearful holders of riches were doing all over Britain, indeed, what people in similar situations had been doing in embattled Gaul for some time. Into a wooden chest—this one embellished with bejeweled gold hinges—they stashed 15 exquisite gold bracelets, three gold necklaces, a three-foot-long gold body chain with a jewel-studded pendant, two gold rings, a silver bowl, several elegant silver figurines, and about 100 beautifully decorated silver spoons and small strainers, some bearing the Greek letters *Chi Rho,* the symbol of Christianity. They then loaded into another container, probably a sturdy cloth bag, more than 1,000 heavy gold solidi coins, 5,000 silver coins, and whatever other valuable items would not fit into the chest. The coins bore images of Honorius, who ruled the western part of the now divided empire and of his brother Arcadius, emperor of the east.

After the sacking of Rome by the Visigoths, ever more hordes of barbarians, including the dreaded Attila and his Huns, rose up to batter away at what was left of the empire. By 476 Italy was ruled by barbarian kings holding court at Ravenna. Italy was reconquered in the sixth century by the Byzantines, who held it until 750. At least half of Britain remained under the control of Britons rather than the barbarians who held most of Europe by 500. But by the end of the fifth century the Saxons had burrowed into the soft underbelly of the island, the key central urban portion, pushing Romanized Britons into Cornwall, Wales, and the north country, where they occupied the old hill forts. How much of Rome's civilization was retained by the weakened Britons is unknown, although it is clear Christianity survived—and with it the Latin language. It was not until 1282 that the last parcel of the Western Empire, hanging on in Wales under a British prince, was surrendered to the Saxon king Edward I.

The Faustini never reclaimed their buried treasure. But since, as aristocratic Roman citizens, they undoubtedly cared deeply about the enduring reputation of their family name, the cached wealth eventually bestowed on them a reward of sorts. One day in 1992 Eric Lawes, a retired British gardener, set out with a metal detector to look for a hammer that had fallen off the tractor of a farmer friend plowing near the Norfolk-Suffolk border. Eventually he found the tool. But first he uncovered a shining gold coin, a solidus, and another coin. Then, as he dug into the earth, he gaped in astonishment at bracelets, necklaces, spoons, and the rest of the amazing Faustini treasure trove. Part of the find lay amid the ruins of the now rotted wooden box; part was piled in the adjacent earth as if a bag that once held it had long since crumbled into powdery soil.

Lawes was stunned by the riches. "This was beyond my wildest dreams," he said. In accordance with British law, he immediately notified museum authorities, who took possession of the golden treasure. Whatever its worth in pounds, the trove offered something more valuable than money—new and tangible evidence of the wealth and style of a long dead world. It was a reminder that even in a remote corner of the empire such as Britain, wealthy people in Roman times had lived urbanely, amid luxurious elegance, and had cherished beauty. And it was, too, a kind of monument to the family that had hidden it, especially as one of the small decorated silver strainers bears the words *Faustine vivas*—Long live Faustini!

A LEGACY PRESERVED IN STONE

Throughout the European territories conquered by its armies, Rome left an indelible mark, a signature in stone that has endured through the centuries: Walls to protect citizens, roads to move troops, aqueducts to supply city dwellers with fresh water, and bridges to leap perilous rivers. As if this were not remarkable enough, much of the building was done by the army, even as the legions were pushing back the empire's frontiers. By Hadrian's time, when Rome was concerned more with consolidation than expansion, the potentially dangerous energies of idle troops far from home and family found outlet in important projects.

In some ways, Roman engineers made European civilization possible. Their achievements in and around Rome had been many. And chief among the public works that benefited the inhabitants most were sewers and aqueducts, both of which, by creating healthy conditions, allowed the population to expand and the city itself to grow. But none of this would have happened without the Roman invention of concrete and the development of the arch as a structural form, and it was these two innovations that the army brought to the empire and put to use everywhere.

Because stone arches could be built to extreme heights—sometimes in double and triple tiers—and shoulder heavy weights, engineers on duty in the provinces could span almost any river or gorge and traverse long distances with solid bridges and towering watercourses. Like many other army-abetted engineering projects, the bridge carrying the aqueduct in Segovia, Spain (*above*), took on giant proportions, reaching 90 feet high and extending 2,700 feet. Built of rough-hewn, uncemented granite blocks, the unusually tall, slender piers and 128 graceful arches still project an image not only of imposing strength but also of a self-confident empire. Dating from AD 100, this engineering marvel has more than withstood the test of time. Until recently it was part of Segovia's water system.

Fear has served as the architect of beauty: and a miraculous change has caused Rome to slough off the old skin of peace, to build towers in haste, and to make all her seven hills to gleam bright again with an unbroken wall." So wrote one Roman of the mighty barriers that were being thrown up around Rome in AD 275 to fend off attack by the Goths. Likewise, cities throughout the empire—many expanded beyond their original walls—made haste to improve their own fortifications.

The construction of city walls was a huge undertaking. Typically, laborers dug two deep ditches around a settlement, heaping the dirt into a high mound between the ditches. This served as the core for two concentric walls. The outer wall, sunk as much as 30 feet below ground level to prevent enemy tunneling, was topped with a broad walk along which soldiers could patrol. The inner wall rose several feet higher, making it more difficult for attackers to fire into the city. And so that they might be all but invulnerable to destruction, the defenses were built up to 20 feet thick, their blocks of stone locked together with metal clamps for additional strength.

Once the walls were completed, construction of the gateways could begin. A temporary wooden arch called a centering was raised over an opening in the wall, upon which skilled masons, working from both sides, placed wedge-shaped stones, known as voussoirs. When the central locking stone, the keystone, was inserted, the centering was moved and another arch begun next to the first. This process was repeated until the entire passageway into the city was covered by a semicircular roof called a barrel vault.

The gatehouses that guarded access to a walled settlement were often small castles in themselves, with soldiers' quarters and stocks of weapons and food. The magnificently preserved Porta Nigra (*right*) in Germany was designed with archery slits instead of ground-floor windows and with rounded towers to give a wider field of fire. In times of siege, its gateways could be blocked with a massive portcullis.

The wall built around Rome in the third century—measuring 12 miles long, 12 feet thick, and 60 feet high—boasted 381 towers and 18 gates with portcullises. Repaired and strengthened, it remained a defense until the advent of artillery in the 19th century. Two-thirds of the wall is still standing.

A relief from Trajan's Column shows helmetless legionaries building a campaign camp with squared pieces of turf during the Dacian wars. The construction of such fortifications was routine practice when Roman soldiers were in hostile territory.

The imposing 100-foot-high Porta Nigra, or Black Gate, stands as a forceful declaration of the might of imperial Rome. Flanked by two towers, one of which has been damaged, the fortified gate provided entry through the second-century walls of the German city of Trier, northern capital of the empire.

One of the most enduring monuments of ancient Rome was the vast network of roads that knitted together the empire's provinces. And while not all of them led directly to Rome, all could trace their heritage to the city, and, specifically, to the Appian Way, the "Queen of Roads." In time, commerce flourished along these arteries. But first and foremost, they were military highways, designed to speed the movement of legions to trouble spots on the frontiers. Not surprisingly, road planning and construction were military affairs.

The laying of a Roman highway began with surveys of extraordinary accuracy. In open territory, roads ran straight, while in broken country they kept to the high ground; where necessary, tunnels carried them through hillsides, and causeways raised them above surrounding marshlands. Surveyors often sighted on fires to align the route, mostly at dawn and at dusk, and to help with their tasks, they also relied on various instruments: a portable sundial to fix directions; a groma, a pole with a horizontal crosspiece from which hung four weighted strings, to measure straight lines and right angles; and a leveling instrument called a chorobates that determined the profile of the land.

Once the engineers had aligned and staked out a route, a plow loosened the earth and marked road margins. Soldiers and laborers then began to dig. Although much depended on the nature of the terrain and the availability of materials, roads typically consisted of several layers. Lime mortar or sand was often laid and tamped down to form a level base, followed by a layer of fist-size stones, sometimes cemented together with mortar or clay. Over this workers laid gravel or coarse sand mixed with hot lime and compacted with a roller. Finally, masons finished the road with paving blocks, built up slightly in the center to form a camber that shed rainwater into side ditches. Because of layering, roads might extend 10 to 15 feet under the pavement, leading some to liken them to walls buried in the ground. They often went 100 years without repair.

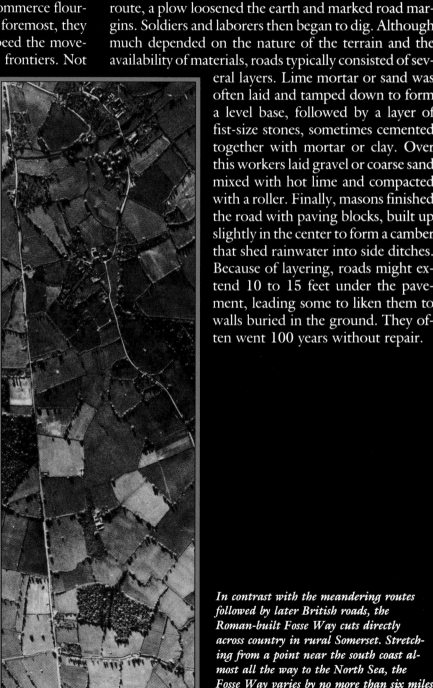

In contrast with the meandering routes followed by later British roads, the Roman-built Fosse Way cuts directly across country in rural Somerset. Stretching from a point near the south coast almost all the way to the North Sea, the Fosse Way varies by no more than six miles out of the same direction.

A Roman road snakes over Wheeldale Moor in North Yorkshire, England. Roads were often built in sections, a mile or so at a time, which may explain the visible changes in their alignment.

A two-wheeled carriage travels along a Roman road toward one of the milestones that dotted the empire. The six-foot cylindrical pillars, frequently weighing more than two tons, usually carried the name of the emperor who had commissioned the road and the distance to the closest provincial town.

Famed for all their engineering accomplishments, the Romans were most proud of the aqueducts that supplied Rome with up to 250 million gallons of fresh water a day. Writing in AD 97, Sextus Julius Frontinus, water commissioner for the city, asked, rhetorically, "Will anybody compare the idle pyramids, or those other useless though renowned works of the Greeks with these aqueducts, these many indispensable structures?" Eventually, 11 aqueducts would deliver to the city water from the southern and eastern hills, elevating engineering to an art in a succession of elegant arches that bounded across the landscape. The Romans were quick to replicate their achievements throughout the empire, and many aqueducts can still be seen in France, Spain, Greece, North Africa, and Asia Minor.

In order to supply provincial cities whose thirsty populations had outgrown local water supplies and to service baths and fountains, engineers constructed channels that tapped rivers and springs that were sometimes dozens of miles distant. Falling at a gentle gradient—a minimum slope of 1 to 200 was recommended by Vitruvius—the precious liquid flowed through covered stone conduits that stretched across the countryside (for the most part in underground tunnels or in trenches that followed the contours of the land) until, finally, it gurgled into public reservoirs safely inside the towns. When the channels had to traverse rivers and gorges, they were raised on arches that maintained the same gradual slope and gave the water a uniform flow.

To ensure consistency in the gradient, surveyors turned once more to the groma and the chorobates, as well as to the diopter, which also measured horizontal angles. Again, much of the expertise in construction lay with the army. In the mid-second century AD, a military engineer was asked to help solve a problem with an aqueduct being built at Saldae, in modern-day Algeria. Two teams of workers had begun to burrow a tunnel through a hill, each starting at opposite sides. The soldier quickly perceived a problem. "I took measurements of both tunnels," he later wrote, "and found that the sum of the two measurements was greater than the width of the hill." The tunnels had missed each other. He solved the problem by boring a hole between the tunnels, uniting them, and allowing the water to flow. The town erected a monument in his honor.

For major building projects, the Romans used cranes such as the one depicted in this second-century AD sepulchral relief. The machine is powered by five men, probably slaves, who work the spokes of the great treadwheel.

When asked to pay for the building of the Pons Fabricius in 62 BC, the Roman Senate demanded proof of the constructed bridge's durability and withheld funds for 40 years. More than two millennia later, the stone bridge is still standing, eloquent testimony to the work of Rome's engineers—and to public money well spent.

The Romans also constructed temporary bridges when necessary, built by soldiers on the march. The simplest of these consisted of a series of boats lashed together and covered with planking. Where a river's current was strong, the army erected a more stable kind of campaign bridge, which was secured by pilings driven down into the riverbed.

With stone bridges, laying foundations for underwater piers posed the greatest challenge. As a first step, engineers created cofferdams, box-shaped watertight enclosures made of wooden pilings and sealed with clay. The cofferdams were driven into the river bottom to surround the proposed site of the foundations, and the water pumped out so that construction could begin. Once the piers reached a height of 30 feet above the river, temporary wooden centerings were hoisted into place between them, and work on the arches started. Masons fitted blocks of stone so accurately cut that they required no mortar, although they were sometimes clamped together with iron. The huge arch stones at Alcántara (*right*) weigh up to eight tons each.

Little remains of one of Rome's finest bridges, however—Trajan's Danube bridge (*below*). Even though Hadrian subsequently dismantled its wooden superstructure in order to prevent access from the enemy's side, the bridge's 20 massive stone piers—each of them 150 feet high and 60 feet wide—were still an awe-inspiring sight. In AD 190, a century after the bridge had been built, the Roman historian Dio Cassius extolled the magnificence of the piers. "They seem to have been erected," he wrote, "for the sole purpose of demonstrating that there is nothing which human ingenuity cannot accomplish."

In a scene from Trajan's Column, the emperor conducts a sacrifice in front of the great bridge he built across the Danube. Nearly three-quarters of a mile long, with 170-foot spans between piers, it boasted a roadway 16 feet wide.

Built in AD 105, the six granite arches of the mighty bridge at Alcántara, in Spain, carry the roadway 170 feet above the Tagus River. Still a crossing point into Portugal, the edifice has lived up to the expectations of its architect, who declared, "I have created a bridge that will last the ages."

A BOLD CLIMB TO GREATNESS

EARLY ROME
753-509 BC

ETRUSCAN WARRIOR

Rome's earliest traditions influenced its later development. Its founder Romulus is said to have created the Senate, choosing 100 city fathers, or patricians, to advise him. Numa Pompilius, the king who followed Romulus, created the priesthoods and religious institutions and gave the Romans their calendar. Tullus Hostilius, his successor, erected the Curia, where the Senate met. The fourth king, Ancus Marcius, constructed the first wooden bridge across the Tiber River. He was followed by three Etruscan kings, represented by the bronze warrior above. Their reigns brought Rome prosperity and construction of the temples to Jupiter, Juno, and Minerva, the city's patron deities. The first Etruscan king, Tarquin I, ruled for 35 years, succeeded by Servius Tullius, who organized a large army.

EARLY REPUBLIC
509-264 BC

TEMPLE OF VESTA

The patricians overthrew the despotic third Etruscan king in 509 BC, creating the republic. In place of kings, they established consuls, two rulers to be elected annually. The masses, or plebs, were granted the right to marry patricians in 445 but were still excluded from the Senate. They elected their own council and officers, who were known as tribunes. Eventually plebs were accepted in religious orders, like the priestesses of the Temple of Vesta, shown above on a gold coin.

Rome fought off conquest by Etruscans, and by the Celts who sacked the city in 390, and organized a defensive league of Latin towns. With armies amplified by recruits from allies, Rome then subdued the Etruscans and the Celts, the highland Samnites, and the Greek colonies of southern Italy and Sicily.

MID-REPUBLIC
264-146 BC

TRIUMPHAL NAVAL COLUMN

Rome was master of Italy as the first of the Punic Wars with the north African city of Carthage began in 264 BC. Control of the Mediterranean by the Carthaginians compelled Rome to build a navy of 100 ships. Its first naval victory over the Carthaginians was commemorated by the column above, decorated with carved anchors and the prows of six captured warships. Although they suffered early losses in sea battles, the Romans eventually triumphed. In 241 they wrested from Carthage control of Sicily, the first Roman province. In the second Punic War, Rome defeated the Carthaginian general Hannibal. At the end of the third Punic War in 146, it annihilated Carthage. Rome then turned eastward, defeating first Syria, then Macedonia, taking over the western part of the Hellenistic world.

LATE REPUBLIC
146-31 BC

IMPERIAL EAGLE

Now in control of the Mediterranean, Rome dominated Spain, North Africa, and the Near East. The spoils of war brought prosperity but also internal upheaval. A popular movement for land reform, led by the brothers Gracchus, was put down by the upper class. Power shifted to the army, whose symbol was the imperial eagle shown above. A series of strong generals transformed Rome into a dictatorship. The first, Gaius Marius, was elected consul seven times. His reforms made the army a professional, highly disciplined force. His erstwhile protégé, Sulla, became dictator of Rome, followed by Pompey the Great, who conquered Jerusalem in 63 BC. He was challenged and defeated by Julius Caesar, who was assassinated in 44, leaving Rome to be ruled by a triumvirate of Caesar's allies.

From its beginnings as an eighth-century BC village of thatched-roof huts, clustered upon the Palatine Hill in Italy, Rome rose to dominate, half a millennium later, most of the Near East, North Africa, and Europe.

Rome (named for its legendary founder Romulus) borrowed traditions from neighboring Greeks and Etruscans, while developing its own culture, which became urban and sophisticated in the imperial era. Its

skilled army Romanized far-off domains, where cities of concrete and marble sprang up to mirror the grand capital. Established by the sword, the empire was largely at peace for almost three centuries.

EARLY EMPIRE
31 BC-AD 68

HIGH EMPIRE
AD 68-235

EMPIRE IN CHAOS
AD 235-305

FALL OF THE WEST
AD 305-565

CARVED GEM

EMPEROR HADRIAN

FOUR TETRARCHS STATUE

HEAD OF CONSTANTINE

The ruling threesome, Mark Antony, Aemilius Lepidus, and Octavian, Caesar's adopted heir, fought among themselves, with Octavian the winner after defeating Antony in a naval battle at Actium. His victory was commemorated on the carved gem above, shown in a plaster impression. Octavian held supreme power as the first emperor, with the title of Augustus. Four of his relatives succeeded him as emperor, among them Claudius, who invaded Britain in AD 43. Twenty-one years later fire ravaged Rome. The emperor Nero, who then reigned, ordered the Christians persecuted. In 66 the Jews of Judea revolted against the harsh Roman rule. Two years later the Spanish legate Galba rebelled against Nero, who committed suicide. Galba declared himself emperor.

Rome was plunged into civil war as army commanders vied to replace Galba as emperor. Galba was murdered by Otho, who was vanquished in turn by Vitellus. Then Vespasian came back from the war in Judea, defeated Vitellus, and seized imperial power. In 70 his son Titus captured Jerusalem. Titus took over from his father, followed by his brother Domitian. The rulers who succeeded him—Trajan, Hadrian, and the Antonine and Severan emperors—governed during a period of unprecedented peace and prosperity, as the empire reached its fullest extent. The marble statue of Hadrian above was found in a temple of Apollo in North Africa, where the Romans built many remarkable structures. Construction in Rome itself included the Baths of Titus, the Colosseum, Trajan's Forum, the Pantheon, and the Baths of Caracalla.

Rome was threatened by corruption at home and military setbacks abroad. In AD 268 the Goths sacked Athens, Corinth, and Sparta. In the absence of a strong ruler, some 20 army leaders, in rapid succession, were named emperor by their troops and then deposed. Christians once again endured harsh persecutions. In time, the emperor Diocletian introduced a series of brilliant reforms that halted the disarray. With the empire besieged from many directions, he saw the value of having two strong leaders: He divided the empire into east and west and appointed an army officer, Maximian, to rule the western part as co-emperor, naming dual successors as well. The ancient statue above, of four tetrarchs, shows Diocletian *(second from the right)*, exhibiting the collegial spirit that the times required.

Constantine the Great defeated his rivals to become sole emperor. He converted to Christianity and established Constantinople as the new capital of the empire. A huge head of Constantine *(above)*, part of a statue, was installed in Rome. After his death, dual emperorships recurred. In AD 363 the Persians seized Mesopotamia. Roman forces battled to hold back the barbarian onslaught from northern Europe. The Goths, led by Alaric, looted Rome in 410. Vandals invaded Gaul and Spain, set up a kingdom at Carthage, and sacked Rome in 455. The Huns under Attila threatened Gaul and Italy but withdrew to the Danube area. Romulus Augustus, the last western emperor, was deposed in 476, and the Ostrogoth king Theodoric took Italy. In the east, the empire flourished until 1453.

ACKNOWLEDGMENTS

The editors wish to thank the following individuals and institutions for their valuable assistance in the preparation of this volume:

Albert Ammerman, Colgate University, Hamilton, New York; Giuseppe Andreassi, Soprintendenza Archeologica della Puglia, Taranto, Italy; Pat Birley, The Vindolanda Trust, Hexham, Northumberland; Robin Birley, The Vindolanda Trust, Hexham, Northumberland; Horst Blanck, Istituto Archeologico Germanico, Rome; Andrea Carandini, Rome; Amanda Claridge, British School at Rome, Rome; Jim Crow, University of Newcastle-upon-Tyne, Newcastle-upon-Tyne; Antonio Di Tanna, Museo della Civiltà Romana, Soprintendenza Comunale alle Antichità e Belle Arti, Rome; Karin Simonsen Einaudi, American Academy in Rome, Rome; Georgia Franzius, Kulturgeschichtliches Museum, Osnabrück, Germany; Mark Hassall, Institute of Archeology, London University, London; Catherine Johns, British Museum, London; Ernst Künzl, Römisch-Germanisches Zentralmuseum, Mainz, Germany; Adriano La Regina, Soprintendenza Archeologica di Roma, Rome; Eugenio La Rocca, Museo della Civiltà Romana, Soprintendenza Comunale alle Antichità e Belle Arti, Rome; Giovanni Lattanzi, Giuliianova, Italy; Eugenio Monti, Rome; Wolfgang Schlüter, Kulturgeschichtliches Museum, Osnabrück, Germany; Valerie Scott, British School at Rome, Rome; Andrew Selkirk, London; Ori Z. Soltes, Klutznick Museum, Washington, D.C.; Susana Tejada, University of Michigan, Ann Arbor; Nicola Terrenato, Rome; Maria Antonietta Tomei, Soprintendenza Archeologica di Roma, Rome; Patricia Weaver, American Academy in Rome, Rome.

PICTURE CREDITS

The sources for the illustrations that appear in this volume are listed below. Credits from left to right are separated by semicolons; credits from top to bottom are separated by dashes.

Cover: © David Harris/courtesy Israel Antiquities Authority. Background Werner Forman Archive, London. End paper: Art by Paul Breeden. 6, 7: Robert L. Vann. 8: © Erich Lessing, Culture and Fine Arts Archive, Vienna. 10: Art by John Drummond, Time-Life Books. 12: Araldo De Luca, Rome—art by John Drummond, Time-Life Books. 13: Scala, Florence—art by John Drummond, Time-Life Books. 14, 15: Barbara Bini, Rome. 16, 17: Alinari/Art Resource, New York. 18: From *Giacomo Boni*, by Luca Beltrami, courtesy British School at Rome; Thomas Ashby Collection, British School at Rome Archive, Rome. 20: Archivio Storico del Museo della Civiltà Romana, Rome. 21: Gianni Dagli Orti, Paris, courtesy Museo della Civiltà Romana, Rome. 23: Scala, Florence. 24: Esther Van Deman series, Photographic Vertical File Collection, Bentley Historical Library, University of Michigan. 27: Photo by James Packer/Museo Nazionale, Rome—rendering by Studio Groma/courtesy James Packer. 28, 29: Carlo Di Pace, Foto-Grafica s.r.l., Rome/Sovraintendenza Comunale, Foro di Traiano, Archivio Fotografico Mercati Traianei e Fori Imperiali, Rome (3)—rendering by Studio Groma/courtesy James Packer. 31: Eberhard Thiem, Lotos Film, Kaufbeuren, Germany. 33-43: Background drawings from Andrea Palladio, *The Four Books of Architecture*, Dover Publications, Inc., New York, 1965. 33: Zefa, London. 34, 35: Marcello Bellisario, Rome. 36: Werner Forman Archive, London. 37: Eugenio Monti, Rome—Eberhard Thiem, Lotos Film, Kaufbeuren, Germany. 38, 39: Dan Budnik/Woodfin Camp/© 1976 Time-Life International BV., from The Great Cities series; Eugenio Monti, Rome. 40, 41: Harten/Schapowalow, Hamburg. 42: From the Resource Collections of the Getty Center for the History of Art and the Humanities. 43: Scala, Florence—Scala/Art Resource, New York. 44: Copyright British Museum, London. 47: Giorgio Nimatallah/Ricciarini, Milan. 49: Photo Jean Mazenod, *L'Art de L'Ancienne Rome*, Éditions Citadelles & Mazenod, Paris. 52, 53: Robert L. Vann. 54: Eberhard Thiem, Lotos Film, Kaufbeuren, Germany/Musei Vaticani, Rome. 56: Scala, Florence. 57: C. M. Dixon, Canterbury, Kent, England. 58: Dmitri Kessel/© 1970 Time-Life Books, from the Library of Art series. 61: Robert L. Vann. 62: Eberhard Thiem, Lotos Film, Kaufbeuren, Germany—from *Hadrian*, by Stewart Perowne, W. W. Norton & Company, Inc., New York, 1961. 63: Zefa, London. 64: Alinari, Florence. 65: Anderson, Florence. 66: Gianni Dagli Orti, Paris/Staatliche Sammlung Ägyptisches Kunstmuseum, Munich. 69: Daniele Amoni, Gualdo Tadino, Perugia, Italy. 70, 71: Gaio Bacci, Rome. 72, 73: Daniele Amoni, Gualdo Tadino, Perugia, Italy. 74, 75: Gaio Bacci, Rome. 76, 77: Eberhard Thiem, Lotos Film, Kaufbeuren, Germany, inset Daniele Amoni, Gualdo Tadino, Perugia, Italy. 78, 79: C. M. Dixon, Canterbury, Kent, England. 80: From *Archeo*, Anno XII, No. 2(84), Feb. 1992, De Agostini/Rizzoli Periodici, Milan. 82: Foto-Grafica s.r.l., Rome/Museo Civico Archeologico, Bologna. 83: Private Collection—Foto-Grafica s.r.l., Rome. 84, 85: Courtesy Archaeological Exploration of Sardis, Harvard University, Cambridge, Mass. 88: Gianni Dagli Orti, Paris/IGDA, Milan. 89: Sonia Halliday Photographs, Weston

BIBLIOGRAPHY

BOOKS

Adam, Jean-Pierre. *La Construction Romaine*. Paris: Grands Manuels Picard, 1984.

Aldred, Cyril. *The Egyptians*. London: Thames and Hudson, 1984.

Ancient Mariners (Seafarers series). Alexandria, Va.: Time-Life Books, 1981.

Bahn, Paul, and Colin Renfrew. *Archaeology: Theories, Methods and Practice*. London: Thames and Hudson, 1991.

Barraclough, Geoffrey. *The Times Atlas of World History*. Maplewood, N.J.: Hammond, 1985.

Birley, Anthony:
Life in Roman Britain. London: B. T. Batsford, 1964.
On Hadrian's Wall. London: Thames and Hudson, 1977.

Boardman, John, Jasper Griffin, and Oswyn Murray (eds.):
The Oxford History of the Classical World. Oxford: Oxford University Press, 1986.
The Roman World. Oxford: Oxford University Press, 1989.

Bowman, Alan K. *The Roman Writing Tablets from Vindolanda*. London: British Museum Publications, 1983.

Breeze, David J., and Brian Dobson. *Hadrian's Wall*. London: Penguin Books, 1976.

Brown, Frank E. *Roman Architecture*. New York: George Braziller, 1986.

Burke, John. *Roman England*. New York: W. W. Norton, 1983.

Campbell, James, Eric John, and Patrick Wormald. *The Anglo-Saxons*. Oxford: Phaidon Press, 1982.

Carcopino, Jérôme. *Daily Life in Ancient Rome: The People and the City at the Height of the Empire*. Translated by E. O. Lorimer. New Haven: Yale University Press, 1940.

Cavendish, Richard (ed.). *Man, Myth and Magic*. London: Marshall Cavendish, 1983.

Coarelli, Filippo. *Monuments of Civilization: Rome*. New York: Grosset & Dunlap, 1972.

Cornell, Tim, and John Matthews. *Cultural Atlas of the World: The Roman World*. Alexandria, Va.: Stonehenge, 1991.

Cottrell, Leonard. *The Great Invasion*. London: Evans Brothers, 1960.

Croft, Peter. *Roman Mythology*. London: Octopus Books, 1974.

Cunliffe, Barry. *Rome and Her Empire*. New York: McGraw-Hill, 1978.

Daniel, Glyn. *A Short History of Archaeology*. London: Thames and Hudson, 1980.

de la Bédoyère, Guy. *The Finds of Roman Britain*. London: B. T. Batsford, 1989.

dell'Orto, Luisa Franchi. *Roma Antica: Vita e Cultura*. Florence: Scala, 1990.

Dudley, Donald R. (trans.). *Urbs Roma*. London: Phaidon Press, 1967.

Dupont, Florence. *Daily Life in Ancient Rome*. Translated by Christopher Woodall. Oxford: Blackwell, 1992.

Ellis, Simon P. "Power, Architecture and Decor: How the Late Roman Aristocrat Appeared to His Guests." In *Roman Art in the Private Sphere*. Edited by Elaine K. Gazda. Ann Arbor: University of Michigan

Press, 1991.

Empires Ascendant (TimeFrame series). Alexandria, Va.: Time-Life Books, 1987.

Empires Besieged (TimeFrame series). Alexandria, Va.: Time-Life Books, 1988.

The Encyclopædia Britannica (Vol. 4). Chicago: Encyclopædia Britannica, 1984.

Ferrill, Arther. *The Fall of the Roman Empire: The Military Explanation.* London: Thames and Hudson, 1986.

Finley, M. I. (ed.). *Atlas of Classical Archaeology.* London: Chatto and Windus, 1977.

Fox, Robin Lane. *Pagans and Christians.* New York: Alfred A. Knopf, 1987.

Gangi, Guiseppe. *Rome: Then and Now.* Rome: G&G Editions, 1985.

Goethe, Johannes W. *Italian Journey, 1786-1788.* Translated by W. H. Auden and Elizabeth Mayer. London: Penguin Books, 1962.

Grant, Michael:
Ancient History Atlas. London: Weidenfeld and Nicolson, 1971 (3d ed.).
The Roman Forum. New York: Macmillan, 1970.

Grant, Michael (ed.). *Greece and Rome: The Birth of Western Civilization.* London: Thames and Hudson, 1986.

Greene, Kevin. *The Archaeology of the Roman Economy.* Berkeley: University of California Press, 1986.

Grimal, Pierre:
In Search of Ancient Italy. Translated by P. D. Cummins. New York: Hill and Wang, 1964.
Roman Cities. Translated and edited by G. Michael Woloch. Madison: University of Wisconsin Press, 1983.

Hadas, Moses. *A History of Rome from Its Origins to 529 A.D. as Told by the Roman Historians.* New York: Doubleday, 1956.

Hadas, Moses, and the Editors of Time-Life Books. *Imperial Rome* (Great Ages of Man series). New York: Time, 1965.

Hall, Jenny, and Ralph Merrifield. *Roman London.* London: Board of Governors of Museum of London, 1986.

Hanfmann, George M. A.:
Letters from Sardis. Cambridge, Mass.: Harvard University Press, 1983.
Sardis: From Prehistoric to Roman Times. Cambridge, Mass.: Harvard University Press, 1983.

Harett, Frederick. *Art: A History of Painting, Sculpture, and Architecture.* New York: Harry N. Abrams, 1976.

Harkabi, Yehoshafat. *The Bark Kokhba Syndrome.* Chappaqua, N.Y.: Rossell Books, n.d.

Henig, Martin (ed.). *A Handbook of Roman Art.* Oxford: Phaidon Press, 1983.

Hodges, Henry. *Technology in the Ancient World.* New York: Alfred A. Knopf, 1970.

Holland, Jack, and John Monroe. *The Order of Rome: Imperium Romanum, Charlemagne and the Holy Roman Empire.* New York: HBJ Press, 1980.

Hooper, Finley. *Roman Realities.* Detroit: Wayne State University Press, 1985.

James, Edward T. (ed.). *Notable American Women, 1607-1950: A Biographical Dictionary.* Cambridge, Mass.: Harvard University Press, Belknap Press, 1974.

Johnson, Paul. *A History of the Jews.* New York: HarperCollins, 1988.

Johnson, Stephen. *English Heritage Book of Hadrian's Wall.* London: B. T. Batsford, 1989.

King, Anthony. *Roman Gaul and Germany.* Berkeley: University of California Press, 1990.

Lambert, Royston. *Beloved and God: The Story of Hadrian and Antinous.* New York: Viking Penguin, 1984.

Lewis, Brenda Ralph. *Growing Up in Ancient Rome.* London: B. T. Batsford, 1980.

Lugli, Giuseppe. *The Roman Forum and the Palatine.* Rome: Bardi Editore, 1961.

Macaulay, David. *City: A Story of Roman Planning and Construction.* Boston: Houghton Mifflin, 1974.

MacDonald, William L.:
The Architecture of the Roman Empire (2 vols.). New Haven: Yale University Press, 1982-1986.
The Pantheon: Design, Meaning and Progeny. London: Penguin Books, 1976.

McKay, A. G. *Houses, Villas and Palaces in the Roman World.* Ithaca, N.Y.: Cornell University Press, 1975.

MacKendrick, Paul. *The Mute Stones Speak.* New York: W. W. Norton, 1983 (2d ed.).

Nash, Ernest. *Pictorial Dictionary of Ancient Rome* (2 vols.). New York: Frederick A. Praeger, 1961-1962 (2d ed.).

The New Illustrated Science and Invention Encyclopedia. Westport, Conn.: H. S. Stuttman, 1989.

Peddie, John. *Invasion: The Roman Invasion of Britain in the Year AD 43 and the Events Leading to Their Occupation of the West Country.* New York: St. Martin's Press, 1987.

Perowne, Stewart. *Hadrian.* New York: W. W. Norton, 1961.

Potter, T. W. *Roman Britain.* London: British Museum Publications, 1984.

Potter, T. W., and Catherine Johns. *Roman Britain.* London: British Museum Press, 1992.

Ragette, Friedrich. *Baalbek.* Parkridge, N.J.: Yoyes Press, 1980.

Ridley, Ronald T. *The Eagle and the Spade.* Cambridge, Mass.: Cambridge University Press, 1992.

The Rise of Cities (TimeFrame series). Alexandria, Va.: Time-Life Books, 1990.

Roman Mosaics. London: Museum of London, 1988.

Rostovzeff, Michael Ivanovitch. *Rome.* Oxford: Oxford University Press, 1960.

Ruggieri, Gianfranco. *The Pantheon.* Rome: Editoriale Museum, 1990.

Scullard, H. H. *Roman Britain: Outpost of the Empire.* London: Thames and Hudson, 1979.

Seaby, H. A. *Roman Silver Coins* (Vol. 2). London: Whitman, 1979 (3d ed.).

Sear, Frank. *Roman Architecture.* Ithaca, N.Y.: Cornell University Press, 1982.

Sorrell, Alan. *Roman Towns in Britain.* London: B. T. Batsford, 1976.

Stambaugh, John E. *The Ancient Roman City.* Baltimore: Johns Hopkins University Press, 1988.

Stillwell, Richard (ed.). *The Princeton Encyclopedia of Classical Sites.* Princeton: Princeton University Press, 1976.

Stobart, J. C. *The Grandeur That Was Rome.* Edited by W. S. Maguinness and H. H. Scullard. London: Sidgwick and Jackson, 1961 (4th ed.).

Suetonius Tranquillus, Gaius. *The Twelve Caesars.* Translated by Robert Graves. Baltimore: Penguin Books, 1957.

Syme, Ronald. *Roman Papers* (Vols. 3 and 6). Edited by Anthony R. Birley. Oxford: Clarendon Press, 1984-1991.

Thébert, Yvon. "Private Life and Domestic Architecture in Roman Africa." In *A History of Private Life* (Vol. 1), edited by Philippe Ariès and Georges Duby. Cambridge, Mass.: Harvard University Press, Belknap Press, 1987.

Vickers, Michael. *Ancient Rome.* Oxford: Phaidon Press, 1989.

Von Hagen, Victor W. *The Roads That Led to Rome.* Cleveland: World Publishing, 1967.

Ward-Perkins, J. B.:
Architecture of the Roman Empire. London: Penguin Books, 1981.
Roman Imperial Architecture: The Pelican History of Art. London: Penguin Books, 1981.

Warry, John. *Warfare in the Classical World.* London: Salamander Books, 1980.

Webster's New Biographical Dictionary. Springfield, Mass.: Merriam-Webster, 1988.

Wells, Colin. *The Roman Empire.* Stanford: Stanford University Press, 1984.

Wheeler, Mortimer. *Roman Art and Architecture.* London: Thames and Hudson, 1964.

White, K. D. *Greek and Roman Technology.* London: Thames and Hudson, 1984.

Wilkes, J. J. *Diocletian's Palace.* Sheffield: University of Sheffield, 1986.

PERIODICALS

Ammerman, Albert J. "Dawn of the Eternal City." *Sciences.* July/August 1989.

Archeo (Milan), February 1989.

Archeo (Milan), June 1990.

Archeo (Milan), October 1992.

Archeo (Milan), November 1992.

Archeologia Viva (Florence), April 1993.

Birley, Robin. "Vindolanda." *Current Archeology* (London), August 1989.

Bower, B. "Early Rome: Surprises Below the Surface." *Science News,* Jan. 14, 1989.

Breeze, David. "Diary: Hadrian's Wall, 1979-1989." *Current Archeology* (London), August 1989.

Connor, Patricia. "Bonanza on the Welsh Border." *Sunday Times* (London), Oct. 24, 1976.

Current Archeology (London), March 1992.

DeLaine, Janet. "Recent Research on Roman Baths." *Journal of Roman Archaeology,* n.d.

Dornberg, John. "Battle of the Teutoberg Forest." *Archaeology,* September/October 1992.

"English Plow Up Roman Gold Trove." *Washington Post,* Nov. 20, 1992.

Erim, Kenan T.:
"Ancient Aphrodisias and Its Marble Treasures." *National Geographic,* August 1967.
"Ancient Aphrodisias Lives Through Its Art." *National Geographic,* October 1981.
"Aphrodisias: Awakened City of Ancient Art." *National Geographic,* June 1972.

Foote, Timothy. "Once Upon a Time These Stones Marked the End of the Civilized World." *Smithsonian,* April 1985.

Ginge, Birgitte. "Ancient Rome." *Archaeology,* 1991.

Hofmann, Paul. "A Few Roads Lead to Carnuntum, Too." *New York Times,* Dec. 23, 1990.

Hofstetter, Eric. "A Late Roman Complex on the Northeast Slope of the Palatine Hill." *Journal of Roman Archaeology,* 1992.

Holder, Paul. "Roman Artillery (I)."
Military Illustrated, August/September 1986.

Journal of Roman Archaeology, Vol. 6, 1993.

Keys, David:
"Timber Palace Found Near Hadrian's Wall." *Times* (London), Summer 1992.
"Treasure Clue to Roman Family." *Independent,* November 20, 1992.

Lattanzi, Giovanni. "Cemetery of Statues." *Archaeology,* November/December 1992.

MacDonald, William L., and Bernard M. Boyle. "The Small Baths at Hadrian's Villa." *Journal of the Society of Architectural Historians,* March 1980.

Marvullo, Joe. "About Photography—The Wall." *Archaeology,* March/April 1987.

Nuttall, Nick, and Norman Hammond. "Experts Reveal Full Glory of Treasure Found in Field." *Times* (London), Nov. 20, 1992.

Packer, James:
"Housing and Population in Imperial Ostia and Rome." *Journal of Roman Studies 67,* 1967.
"Politics, Urbanism, and Archaeology in 'Roma Capitale.'" *American Journal of Archaeology 93,* 1989.
"Restoring Trajan's Forum." *Inland Architect,* September/October 1990.

"Pieces of a Puzzle." *ARTnews,* January 1991.

Pinto, John. "Pastoral Landscape and Antiquity: Hadrian's Villa." *Studies in the History of Art* (National Gallery of Art, Washington, D.C.), Vol. 36, 1992.

Quattrocchi, Giovanna. "I Bronzi di Rabat." *Archeo* (Milan), February 1992.

Ridgway, Francesca. "A Summary of Papers Presented at the Second National Etruscan Conference." *Journal of Roman Archaeology,* Vol. 5, 1992.

Speidel, Michael A. "Roman Soldiers' Pay." *Minerva,* July/August 1993.

Turner, Jonathan. "Rome: Pieces of a Puzzle." *ARTnews,* January 1991.

Watts, Donald J., and Carol Martin Watts. "A Roman Apartment Complex." *Scientific American,* December 1986.

OTHER SOURCES

"Archeologia a Roma Nelle Fotografie di Thomas Ashby, 1891-1930." Catalog. British School at Rome.

Birley, Robin. *Roman Vindolanda.* Illustrated guide. Hexham, Northumberland: Vindolanda Trust, n.d.

Capitoline Museums, Rome (Practical Guides—English). Milan: Federico Garolla, 1984.

Conners, Joseph. "Introduction." American Academy Catalog, 1991.

"Domus: A Late Roman Mansion." *Alumni Newsletter* of the College of Fine and Applied Arts, Urbana: University of Illinois, 1991-92.

Patricius, Petrus. "Excerpta e Petri Patricii Historia." *National Union Catalog Pre-1956 Imprints,* Vol. 453.

Scott, Russell T. "From the Palatine." *Bulletin of the American Academy in Rome,* n.d.

Vann, Lindley. "Hadrian's Villa." Notes taken of Frank Brown lecture on Hadrian's Villa, n.d.

INDEX

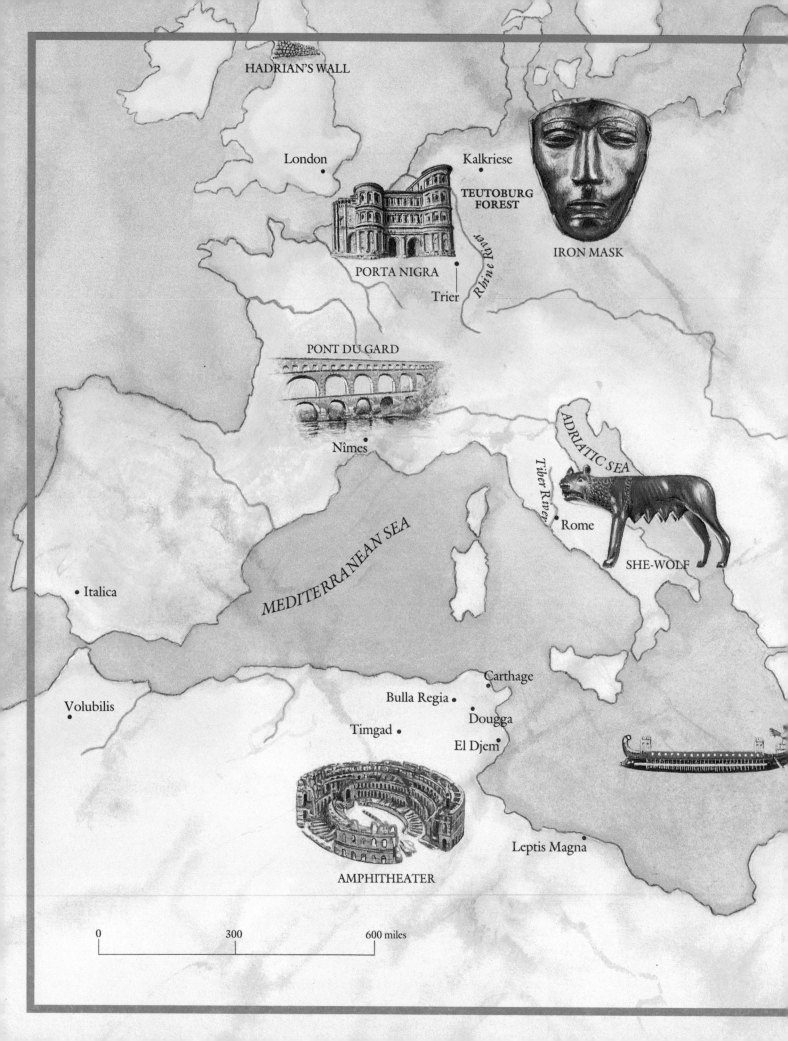

HADRIAN'S WALL

London

Kalkriese

TEUTOBURG
FOREST

IRON MASK

PORTA NIGRA

Trier

Rhine River

PONT DU GARD

Nîmes

ADRIATIC SEA

Tiber River

Rome

SHE-WOLF

MEDITERRANEAN SEA

Italica

Volubilis

Carthage

Bulla Regia

Dougga

Timgad

El Djem

Leptis Magna

AMPHITHEATER

0   300   600 miles